T0160936

Mayflower

THE VOYAGE FROM HELL

Mayflower

THE VOYAGE FROM HELL

KEVIN JACKSON

London and New York

Mayflower: The Voyage from Hell
9 8 7 6 5 4 3 2 1

First published by TSB 2020

Published in 2021 in the United States by
Leapfrog Press Inc.
P.O. Box 1293
Dunkirk, New York 14048

Distributed in the United States by
Consortium Book Sales and Distribution
St. Paul, Minnesota 55114
www.cbsd.com

All rights reserved under International and
Pan-American Copyright Conventions

© 2020 Kevin Jackson
Author portrait: © Marzena Pogorzały
www.marzenapogorzaly.com

The moral right of Kevin Jackson to be identified as the author of this work
has been asserted by him in accordance with the Copyright, Designs and
Patents Act 1988.

All rights reserved. No portion of this book may be reproduced, stored in a
retrieval system or transmitted in any form, or by any means, electronic,
mechanical, photocopying, recording or otherwise, except brief extracts for the
purpose of review, without the prior written permission of the publisher.

Cover, text and map design: James Shannon
Set in Adobe Garamond Pro and 1689 GLC Garamond Pro

ISBN: 978-1-948585-163 (paperback)

Printed and bound in the United Kingdom by TJ Books Ltd

About the Author – Kevin Jackson

Kevin Jackson was an English writer, broadcaster and film-maker. He had also been a Teaching Fellow of Vanderbilt University, Nashville; a radio producer and television director for the BBC; Associate Arts Editor for *The Independent* and a roving reporter for *Night and Day* Magazine, where his assignments included a week on a fishing boat in Atlantic waters, a training mission on a Royal Navy aircraft carrier and a helicopter flight to an oil rig in the Caspian, near Baku. His books include *Constellation of Genius* (Hutchinson), a history of modernism which was a Book of the Week in *The Guardian* and a Book of the Year in the *Express*; *Invisible Forms* (Picador); *Carnal* (Pallas Athene); and the authorized biography *Humphrey Jennings* (Picador). He collaborated with the cartoonist Hunt Emerson on several projects, including *Bloke's Progress* (Ruskin Comics), a comic fable inspired by the writings of John Ruskin; a version of Dante's *Inferno* (Knockabout); and, most recently, *Lives of the Great Occultists* (Knockabout). His long narrative poem, *Greta and the Labrador* (Holland House Books) was charmingly illustrated by the artist Jo Dalton. Jackson's other regular collaborators included the cameraman Spike Geilinger, who shot most of his independent films, and the musician Colin Minchin, with whom he co-wrote the rock opera *Bite*. He was a Fellow of the Royal Society of Arts, a Companion of the Guild of St George, and a Regent of the Collège de 'Pataphysique. At his untimely death, Kevin Jackson had completed four of the titles in his Seven Ships Maritime History series. We hope to publish Captain Cook's *Endeavour* in due course. Though each volume tells an independent tale, the series also charts the rise and decline of Britain as the world's greatest naval power.

TSB | Can of Worms will proudly publish Kevin Jackson's wonderful homage to TE Lawrence: *Legion: Thirteen Ways of Looking at Lawrence of Arabia* in 2022. Many moving obituaries were published shortly after Kevin Jackson's death, and links can be found at: www.canofworms.net/KevinJackson.

Production and Publishing Credits

A considerable number of people are involved in realizing an author's work as a finished book on the shelf of your local library, bookshop or online retailer. TSB would like to acknowledge the critical input of:

Cover design, layout and cartography. TSB/Can of Worms has benefited from a longstanding relationship with James Shannon on book production and website development for many of its own titles as well as some of Can of Worms's consultancy clients. For this *Seven Ships Maritime History* Series, James has undertaken the cover design, page layout as well as map design. James and further examples of his work can be found at: www.jshannon.com

Editorial. Editorial has been provided by Tobias Steed, publisher of TSB/Can of Worms. Tobias's career in publishing has spanned forty plus years having started as an editorial assistant for Johns Hopkins University Press in Baltimore, co-founder of illustrated travel guides publishing company, Compass American Guides, Oakland, California, Associate Publisher and Director of New Media at Fodor's/Random House, New York, and most recently founder and publisher of Can of Worms Enterprises Ltd. www.canofworms.net

Ship Plans. Permission for the use of the ship plans in the *Seven Ships Maritime History* series* have been provided to TSB/Can of Worms by Vadiim Eidlin at Best Ship Models, a company that provides accurate ship plans designed especially for model shipbuilders. Their collection includes 500+ plans for beginners and professional modelers. www.bestshipmodels.com

*the plans used in *Darwin's Odyssey: The Voyage of the Beagle* are from Alamy.com

Sales and Marketing. Sales and Marketing. Sales and Marketing for the Seven Ships Maritime History and all other Leapfrog Press titles is overseen by Consortium Book Sales and Distribution (CBSD) St. Paul, Minnesota 55114 www.cbsd.com

Publicity. All publicity enquiries should be directed to Mary Bisbee-Beek. leapfrog@leapfrogpress.com. Further information and resources for the Seven Ships Maritime History series can be found at www.leapfrogpress.com

Seven Ships Maritime History Series – a Note from the author

In the summer of 2006, about five years before the Syrian Civil War began, I spent a couple of weeks in Damascus. In theory I was doing some informal research about Lawrence of Arabia, but in reality I mostly wandered the streets and gazed at the buildings and was touched by the exquisite good manners of the local people. In the afternoons, when the heat became oppressive for a pale European, I went into the Umayyad Mosque – infidels are quite welcome there – and squatted next to one of the pillars, and read the book I had brought with me: a hardback edition of Livingstone Lowes' *The Road to Xanadu,* which is a wonderful exploration of all the travel narratives that fed the imagination of the young Coleridge. It was delicious to escape from the uncomfortable warmth of a Damascene summer and daydream about the snow and the icebergs and the dark, chill waters that the ancient mariners had met when they ventured to the far north.

The extracts from old diaries and letters and memoirs cited in this study re-awoke in me that sense of wonder which the best sailors' tales have always inspired, especially in children. When I put the book down to daydream, I began to think of how fascinating it would be for me to find out more about maritime history, and to tell the stories of the greatest British ships over the centuries of the Western maritime expansion. It was not hard to choose seven famous vessels for seven books, each of which would have its own major themes: *Golden Hind* (exploration, plunder), *Mayflower* (religion, emigration), *Endeavour* (science, colonialism), *Bounty* (rebellion, survival), *Victory* (war, heroism), *Beagle* (biology, genius) and *Endurance* (leadership, heroism, survival). Each volume would be self-contained, but would also mark a chapter in the rise and decline of British maritime power and the creation of the modern world.

The idea came to me whole, in a single dreamy afternoon, and I knew it was what I wanted to do next. Now all I had to do was write my tales: the stories of Seven Ships.

Kevin Jackson, 2020

Table of Contents

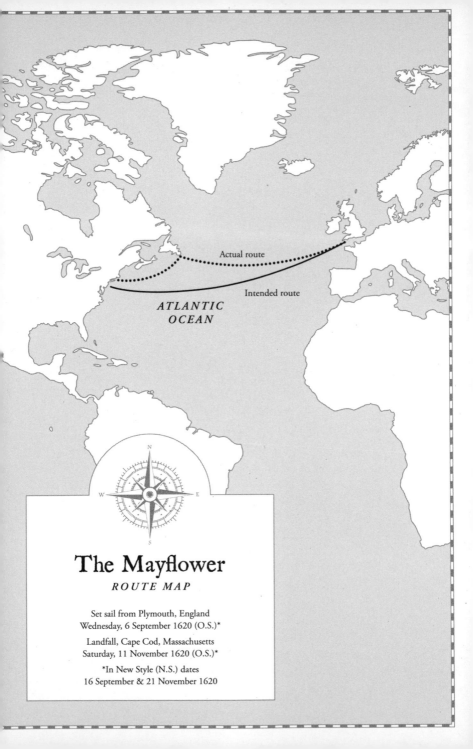

ATLANTIC
OCEAN

Actual route

Intended route

The Mayflower
ROUTE MAP

Set sail from Plymouth, England
Wednesday, 6 September 1620 (O.S.)*

Landfall, Cape Cod, Massachusetts
Saturday, 11 November 1620 (O.S.)*

*In New Style (N.S.) dates
16 September & 21 November 1620

Chapter One

September 1620 : The Voyage

I t was already perilously late in the year for a westward Atlantic crossing. The leaking *Speedwell* had been forced twice to turn back before the ships had reached Plymouth from Southampton. This smaller companion vessel, meant to accompany the emigrants across the ocean, would now leave *Mayflower* to make a solo voyage. The journey should have taken place during the summer months of calmer seas and clearer skies but delays and mishaps had kept *Mayflower* in Plymouth, the most south-westerly major sailing port in the English mainland, until early autumn. She finally sailed out of Plymouth, alone, on Wednesday, 6 September 1620, and the Atlantic crossing would take nine and a half weeks: sixty-seven terrible days.

A spring or summer voyage would have taken about half that time, and had they been able to afford the expense of waiting in Plymouth for six months, the travellers would have been well advised to postpone their journey until the late spring of 1621. But funds were low, dreadfully low, and provisions lower still. They simply could not afford to wait any longer. Either sail now, or give up the attempt and go home, penniless.

At first the winds were kind to the *Mayflower*, and progress steady. Even so, life on board was at best uncomfortable.

Picture her. She was by no means a large vessel: the most accurate calculations show that she was just 90 feet from stempost to sternpost, with a keel of 58 feet, a breadth of 25-26 feet and a depth of twelve and a half feet. She was registered as 181 tons, meaning that her hold was large enough to contain that quantity of wine or rum packed in barrels.

Put this another way: she was only about twelve feet longer than a tennis court. And she had not been designed as a passenger ship, but for cargo. Until recently, she had been sailing back and forth across the English Channel, plying the wine trade and bringing to England the delicious products of Bordeaux. This made her a so-called "sweet ship" – not foul-smelling like those vessels which carried more noxious cargoes.

The main deck was 75 feet by 20 feet, but a good part of this was occupied by the "shallop" – a sturdy open rowing boat, about thirty-three feet long by 9 wide, with a draught of three feet. This vessel would be invaluable to them once they had made their crossing, but for the duration it had been cut into sections that would be reassembled on land. They also had a smaller longboat and another smaller rowing boat.

102 passengers and about 25-30 crew shared the voyage with these three bulky boats, and they would have been cramped even without them. And apart from the short periods when they were allowed up on deck for a little

exercise and sun – not too often, for the crew had plenty of work to do round the clock, and they were often rude to the landlubbers – the passengers mostly spent their time in the almost complete darkness that prevailed below deck, relieved here and there by the odd candle or the flames of the Fire Box, a precariously balanced metal contraption with a sand tray. Everyone took turns to cook their frugal meals in small groups of three or four. *Mayflower*'s captain and master, Christopher Jones, had a small cabin at the after end of the half-deck, and his two officers had smaller berths of their own, but the crew and passengers had to rough it as best they could.

Anyone more than five feet tall would have to crouch or crawl when clambering around below deck which was built to store barrel. This space, in which most of them tried to live as healthy a life as possible, measured 25 feet by 15 feet at its largest point. It provided the 102 passengers with less than four square feet per person – about the size of a single bed, or a coffin. Here they slept, prepared food, cared for children, changed clothes and attempted to maintain some level of privacy. This was unpleasant even when the *Mayflower* was safely at anchor. Out in the open seas, it was a chamber of torments.

England fell behind them. During the first weeks of September, the waves were more than high enough to make the ship roll and pitch, and though the crewmen had their sea legs and were mainly unaffected, most of the passengers fell ill with seasickness almost at once. Only callous souls, or those who have never suffered the malady, will make light of seasickness, which at best is a state of utter physical and mental misery, and at worst can be fatal.

One of the passengers, William Bradford, kept notes on

the journey which he later used as the basis for his history *Of Plymouth Plantation*, a narrative which has sometimes been called the earliest work of American literature. The section of the work devoted to the ocean journey is tantalisingly brief – just a few paragraphs in Chapter Nine – so it is all the more striking that Bradford goes out of his way to comment on the early onset of seasickness among his people.

But professional sailors can be a cruel bunch, and one of the younger *Mayflower* hands delighted in coming below deck, loudly mocking the afflicted, confidently predicting that at least half of them would surely die, and describing in morbid detail how he would take pleasure in chucking their bodies overboard and making free with their possessions.

The young bully soon had cause to regret his cruelty. Less than half-way through the trip, he fell ill with some unspecified disease – possibly a ruptured appendix – and was himself given a sea burial. As Bradford noted, this was taken as a sign of divine anger: "Thus his curses light on his own head, and it was an astonishment to all his fellows for they noted it to be the just hand of God upon him." The teasing died down after this.

But the blight of seasickness persisted, and it was made worse by the ship's primitive means of sanitation, which at its most hygienic was also at its most perilous: small, open-bottomed boxes which could be balanced precariously on the ship's rail. It took courage or extreme fastidiousness to risk using these, and for the most part, the voyagers did as countless others have done across the ages: they threw slops overboard from wooden buckets.

What could not be thrown overboard would seep down into the ballast to join the sewage that was already decaying there. Before long, all but the most hardened sailors were refusing to go down below and pump out the bilge. The people of Elizabethan and Jacobean England were far less fastidious than their descendants, but even they found conditions on board disgusting. As with all ships of the period, the hold was also teeming with cockroaches and rats. If she had once been a sweet ship, she was now a floating slum.

Half-way across the ocean, the crosswinds came, and with them the fierce storms. On 22 September, one of the company led his fellow passengers in the Psalm for the day. It was an ominously appropriate text:

> They that go down to the sea in ships and
> occupy by the great waters. They see the
> works of the Lord, and his wonders in the
> deep. For he commandeth and raiseth the
> stormy wind, and it lifteth up the waves
> thereof. They mount up to the heaven
> and descend to the deep, so that their soul
> melteth for trouble. They are tossed to and
> fro and stagger like a drunken man, for all
> their cunning is gone.

The agonies were many. First there was the constant fear of death by drowning. During storms – and from now on the storms came hard and fast – *Mayflower* was tossed around wildly. All the crew could do was to "hull" – that is, to bring down the sails and surrender to the elements. For day after day she would have been sailing with almost bare poles, with just a storm trysail to keep her pointed across the waves.

Torrential rains and battering winds could spring up

as if out of nowhere, and the task of swiftly lowering the boat's heavy sails, arduous at the best of times, became intensely dangerous in a turbulent sea. Above all, the men had to protect the bowsprit and the spritsail, which could be ripped off and swallowed by the waves. Crewmen slithered across the slippery decks, which flew up and plunged down below their bare feet. At any second they might be thrown overboard.

Astonishingly only one man, a 27-year-old named John Howland, servant to John Carver, suffered this usually fatal accident; still more astonishingly, he survived it. As the ship lurched and he flew through the air, he managed to grab hold of a rope, and to cling to it doggedly. As William Bradford related it,

> It pleased God that he caught hold of the
> topsail halyards which hung overboard
> and ran out at length. Yet he held his hold
> (though he was sundry fathoms under
> water) till he was hauled up by the same
> rope to the brim of the water, and then with
> a boat hook and other means got into the
> ship again and his life saved.

Howland brought up pint after pint of salt water, and was ill for many days, but he completed the crossing and lived on in the New World to the ripe age of eighty.

Bringing in the sails was not the only urgent chore. Giant walls of water would smash into *Mayflower*'s sides, peeling aside the wood, punching holes in the hull which had to be repaired and then smothered with hot pitch before the leaking became too bad – bad enough, that is, to sink her. The heavy seas made the timbers of the shop "work" – or open slightly at the seams – and it was all but impossible to stop rivulets of cold water from running down into the cabins, soaking everyone to the skin. The passengers huddled in their wet bedding, salt water streaming down the cabin walls, and prayed for deliverance.

Though they were exposed to more immediate dangers than the passengers, the crew were the fortunate ones. They had their urgent tasks to carry out, and they were hardened mariners.

The constant noise was another torment. A powerful storm can be alarming enough on land, but at sea the air is torn with the sounds of wind screaming through the rigging, the crashing of water against timber just feet or even inches away, and the sickening groaning of the hull as the elements battered it. At night, the terrors were all the greater.

And then came the other, opposite affliction: dead calm. For a while, these quiet days came as a blessed relief. On the mornings when the wind finally dropped and the waters grew placid, the passengers would crawl up from their sodden quarters to dry their clothes and bedding. But too long a period becalmed had dangers of its own. Supplies were dwindling and already some passengers were falling sick with scurvy, caused by vitamin C deficiency, the universal hazard of long voyages. Which was better: a swift death by water or a slow death by starvation? The sailors had their traditional spells and superstitions to raise the wind: they would whistle loudly, or stick a knife in the mainmast, or – a last resort – make a crewman clamber out along the mainstay and tie an old boot on it. Did they really believe these rituals had any power over the elements? No matter. The storms returned and now they were worse than ever.

Saints and Strangers

Who were these tormented people? Why had they voluntarily given themselves over to such hardship and hazard?

They were English of the middling sort, neither conspicuously wealthy (though some had been successful merchants) nor desperately poor (though some of them knew what it was to go hungry). Not all of them were literate. Quite a few of them came from old farming families in the Midland and East Anglia, and so were provincials. They would not have fully understood what they were letting themselves in for.

The senior passengers had reached adulthood under Queen Elizabeth. James I was monarch of England now, and had been since 1603, but culturally these people and their children remained Elizabethans, and shared some of the better qualities of that paradoxical age of exquisite delicacy and abominable cruelty, civility and mayhem, filth and splendour. At their best, they were adventurous, principled, selfless, robust and brave.

They fell into two groups: the Saints (or in the spelling of their day, "Saincts"), ideological, theological migrants and the Strangers, who had compelling reasons of their own for risking their lives at sea. Few if any of the Strangers were driven by a calling to spread the Gospel; for the most part they simply hoped that they would fare better in the new world.

The Saints did have strong religious motives. They wished to practise their Separatist faith – that is, to be separate from the established Church of England which they regarded as corrupt and Catholic – and if possible to convert the heathen "salvages" – or Indians, as they were also known. The Separatists had long proclaimed to all who would listen that the Roman Catholic Church was an instrument of Satan and this, to them, was not just aggressive rhetoric, but plain and literal truth.

Popular history has made a caricature of these determined souls. For one thing, they did not call themselves Pilgrims (that term was not widely used until about 1840). Nor were they fleeing immediate persecution. Until very recently, most the Saints had been living peacefully in the tolerant city of Leyden, in the Low Countries.

The received myth of the Pilgrims confuses these folk with the Massachusetts Bay Puritans who came to America about ten years later and settled about fifty miles to the north of Plymouth Plantation. So we tend to picture our band of Pilgrims dressed all in black, with high pointy hats. In reality, they were not at all enemies of "gay apparel", and, except on Sundays when black dress was compulsory, mostly wore garments of russet or dark green, though the women sometimes wore quite handsome dresses of saffron or dark blue, with fairly low necks and white collars.

The Pilgrims had firm principles, but they lacked the note of intransigent fanaticism that the worst of the Puritans brought to America. They were humane and compassionate both to each other and to the Strangers, and their successors at Plymouth would not go on to hunt and execute witches nor to hang Quakers. They were much given to ferocious disputes, among themselves as well as with others, and some of them were masters of blisteringly aggressive rhetoric. They were not democratic in ways that we would recognise, yet there was much in their way of thinking and of conducting their affairs that would establish a movement towards democracy in the new land. They were serious, but not sanctimonious or censorious.

They enjoyed their beer (the essential daily drink of all English people from childhood on, as it was far safer than most water), their wines and their "strong waters" (gin and brandy). Though they were admirably slow to complain of their lot, it is worth noting that the Pilgrims grumbled loudly when supplies of proper drink grew low and they were forced to take their liquid refreshment from ponds and streams.

They also ate heartily when it was possible, with appetites that to us sound enormous. Even when *Mayflower* was still half-way across the Atlantic, the diet was hefty if monotonous. Each adult person was issued with a daily allowance of a pound of ship's biscuit, a pound of butter, and half a pound of cheese, all to be washed down with a gallon of (weak) ale. In addition, each passenger was given two pounds of salt beef or pork every week, as well as a ration of salted cod and dried peas.

One other (now mostly forgotten) detail: several of those who had played a major part in the story had all originally came from a quiet Nottinghamshire village, with a wholly unheroic name for the birthplace of heroes – Scrooby.

Chapter Two

Men of Scrooby: 1603 – 1608

S crooby is a modest village in the northern part of the
county of Nottinghamshire, a short ride away from
the legendary home of Robin Hood and his men, Sher-
wood Forest. It has only ever had one building of any
distinction: Scrooby Manor, by all accounts a handsome
house – some referred to it as a "palace" – with thirty
bedrooms, a private chapel and a moat. The house was
owned by the Archbishopric of York, which allowed it to
fall into disuse and disrepair until it was finally abandoned
in 1637.

One of the ruined walls bears a plaque. It recalls that in
this place had been the home of

In this place had been the home of
William Brewster
From 1588 to 1608, and where he organized the
Pilgrim Church, of which he became the ruling elder
And with which, in 1608, he removed to

Amsterdam,
In 1609 to Leyden, and in 1620 to Plymouth, where
He died.
April 16, 1644.

The bare bones of this statement need a little re-setting and fleshing out. Young William Brewster had in fact been brought to live in Scrooby Manor as early as 1575, when his father – also called William – was appointed as "bailiff-receiver" (that is, rent collector) of the Manor, responsible for gathering payments from the surrounding villages. The role was modestly paid, but allowed him full use of the Manor and its surroundings.

At the very start of December 1580, the 15-year-old Brewster set off by horse for Cambridge. On 5 December, he signed the matriculation rolls at Peterhouse, the oldest of Cambridge's colleges, at that time fourteen in number.

Cambridge was not, in Elizabeth's time, the highly respected seat of learning it would become in later centuries. In some circles it was notorious for the idleness and cynicism of its dons and the delinquent behaviour of its students, many of whom spent more time drinking, gambling or whoring than in study. The colleges were condemned as the "haunts of drones, the abodes of sloth and luxury, monasteries whose inmates yawn and snore... leading their lives in vanity, folly, and idleness."

But even the most slothful universities may become the seed-beds of rebellion; and Cambridge was becoming just such a university – a place where clever, ardent, angry young men could gather to discuss dangerous new ideas. Most rebellions have need of a charismatic leader, and the man under whose influence Brewster fell was the Reverend Robert Browne, a graduate of Corpus Christi College.

Browne so antagonised the university town with his radical sermons that he was forced to decamp to the city of Norwich, where he began to hold private meetings attended by a "vulgar sort of people... to the number of one hundred at a time." The Bishop of Norwich promptly had him jailed; he was soon released on appeal to a powerful relative but the Bishop immediately had Browne arrested and imprisoned again.

Eventually, Browne and his followers fled England and settled in Holland. It was here that Browne wrote two works which had an immense influence on religion and society for centuries to come: *A Treatise of Reformation without Tarying for Anie*, and *A Booke which Sheweth the Life and Manner of all True Christians*. (1582). These two works provided the intellectual foundations of the Pilgrim Church, and the American Congregational Church which grew from it.

The teaching of St Paul supplied Browne with his pattern of Christian conduct: "Come out from among them, and be ye separate, saith the LORD, and touch not the unclean thing". *Be ye separate*. Worthy souls should withdraw from the establish Church and form small unions which would covenant to "forsake and deny all ungodliness and wicked fellowship." These groups would operate on a democratic basis, choose their own pastors and live the lives of "saincts".

Browne was eventually to grow disillusioned with his own teachings, recant, and discreetly rejoin the Church of England. But his defection did not deter others – like the young Brewster – from following Browne's teachings. Eventually, that is. For the next few years, Brewster lived quite a grand and even adventurous life in the service of Sir William Davison, a shrewd and powerful minster, admired and trusted by Elizabeth herself.

Brewster joined Sir William in London, where he worked hard for his employer, who liked the Cambridge alumnus so well that, as was enviously remarked, he treated Brewster more like a son than a servant. Brewster was being groomed for a dazzling career in diplomacy, but then it all came tumbling down.

Elizabeth wanted Mary Queen of Scots to be executed, but she did not wish that deadly intention to be known. A scapegoat was needed. Luckily for Elizabeth, Davison had been negligent in his supervision of the royal prisoner, and she put it about that Davison had exceeded his powers. In 1587 Davison was tried for contempt, found guilty and sent to the Tower of London for two years. The loyal Brewster stayed with him throughout, trying to make his life as comfortable as possible. Then, on Davison's release, he made his way back to Scrooby.

Here, Brewster found plenty of business to occupy and console him. His father died just a year later, in 1590; he inherited both his father's positions, and enjoyed moderate wealth. He took a wife, Mary, and on 12 August 1593 she gave birth to the first of his children, Jonathan. He seemed to be a happy man, and a good neighbour, held in "esteem among them, especially the godly and religious".

Brewster's new friends in his old home included one Richard Clyfton, the rector of the parish of Babworth, which lies about six miles from Scrooby. Nominally still an Anglican, Clyfton was in fact winning respect among pious locals as a "grave and reverent" preacher of reforming ways. William and Mary Brewster fell into the habit of walking to Babworth every Sunday to hear Clyfton's words of wisdom.

King James's persecution of heretical Christians was growing ever more severe. Greater secrecy was needed, and, largely at William Brewster's suggestion, those who lived in and nearby Scrooby would hold their meetings in private places – most often in Scrooby Manor itself. Richard Clyfton, at the grand old age of fifty now rather an Old Testament prophet, came to act as their pastor. These meetings were not large – they were usually attended by about thirty or forty people. Soon, they noticed a new face among their number – a man of modest demeanour, though of good education. This was John Robinson.

Mr John Robinson

Soon after he heard news of James' coronation in 1603, a young clergyman by the name of John Robinson (born in about 1576, and so not yet thirty years old) resigned his living at St. Andrew's, Norwich, because he refused to subscribe to the Thirty-Nine Articles. One of the articles condemned Separatism; and Robinson could not agree to this.

Robinson, evidently, was a man of stern principle. Like William Brewster, he had been educated at Cambridge University; unlike Brewster, who left without taking a degree, he had gone on to become a fellow of Corpus Christi College. He married a local woman, Bridget White, by whom he had three children: John the younger, Bridget the younger, and Isaac.

They settled in a village on the banks of the river Trent,

Gainsborough. About twelve miles away was a smaller village: Scrooby, where Robinson was now in regular attendance. In spite of his self-effacing manner, Robinson's intelligence and learning made him one of the most admired and well-loved men in the congregation. He was accepted as Clyfton's unofficial second-in-command.

It was as well that the attendants at Scrooby Manor had such powerful characters among them, because the crackdown on Separatists was coming. In 1607, the authorities raided. As William Bradford, the historian of Plymouth Plantation, later wrote:

> They were hunted and persecuted on every
> side. Their former afflictions were but as
> flea-bitings in comparison with these which
> now came upon them. For some were
> taken and clapped up in prison, others had
> their houses beset and watched day and
> night, and most were fain to flee and leave
> their houses and habitations, and the means
> of their livelihood.

Mrs Brewster gave birth to a daughter at this time. They called her "Fear".

On the last day of September 1607, Brewster finally resigned his secular positions as Bailiff and Postmaster. A few months later, he and some of his friends were summoned to York to face the Court of High Commission. They were each fined £20 for being "disobedient in matters of religion". Not, perhaps, the most horrifying of penalties, but for the faithful of Scrooby it was the final humiliation.

They began to speak of fleeing to Holland. As Bradford

recalled years later:

> Seeing themselves thus molested, and that
> there was no hope of their continuance
> there, by a joint consent they resolved to
> go into the Low Countries, where they
> heard was freedom of religion for all men:
> as also how sundry from London and other
> parts of the land, had been exiled and
> persecuted for the same cause, and were
> gone thither, and lived at Amsterdam, and
> in other places of the land.

So their first flight from persecution was not to be a long
haul across the ocean, but a short sail to Holland.

British Colonies

The Atlantic voyage of *Mayflower* voyage was not the first
British trip to the New World. Henry VII had financed
two expeditions in 1497 and 1498, which grabbed Chesa-
peake Bay and Newfoundland for His Majesty. But it was
not until the last quarter of the sixteenth century, under
Elizabeth, that England set about a more systematic and
determined settlement of the New World. It was Elizabeth's personal astrologer and court magus, Dr John Dee,
who coined the term "British Empire".

At first, the whole colonial enterprise seemed doomed
to failure. A brief attempt to create a settlement in
Newfoundland soon collapsed. In a more notorious disas-

ter, Sir Walter Raleigh established a colony on Roanoke Island, Virginia in 1587, and left 150 settlers there. When the English ships returned in 1591, not a soul was found.

But a later Virginian venture came to fare reasonably well. Jamestown was founded in 1607 and named after the new king, who in 1606 had granted the London Company the rights to colonise America between the 38th and 41st parallels: roughly, from present-day Virginia to New Jersey. The first years were grim: the Native Americans of the region were hostile and given to murderous attacks, the swamps gave birth to dreadful outbreaks of malaria and other illnesses, and the supplies they brought from England began to run out.

Still, with the help of Captain John Smith, a core of the settlers survived. Eventually they were able to form a stable and well-regulated community. Not, though, the kind of community that would have seemed attractive to voyagers on *Mayflower*, since most of the Jamestown folk were loyal to their King and to the Church – the Church of England. The pilgrims did not merely disapprove of that Church: they feared it, and the monarch who was now enforcing its tenets so fiercely.

King James purges his Church

The most recent of the major historical events to precipitate the voyage of the *Mayflower* was the coronation of King James in 1603. Elizabeth, the Virgin Queen, was dead at last, and Tudor rule of England died with her. James belonged to the unhappy House of Stuart, whose command would be temporarily overthrown during the English Revolution and finally abolished in the so-called "Glorious Revolution" of 1688 which brought the House of Hanover to the throne.

Both Catholics and Protestants had high hopes of the new regime, and both would be disappointed. Some 800 Church of England ministers – about a tenth of the Anglican clergy – presented James with a document which came to be known as the Millenary Petition, begging their monarch to put an end to many of what they saw as the worst abuses of those Anglican priests who held fast to the old Catholic ways: widespread laxity in the keeping of the Sabbath, the inclusion of the Apocrypha in the Bible, the sparseness of weekly sermons by those competent to preach, and, as usual, the continued used of "papish" vestments.

In response, James called the Hampton Court Conference in 1604. The meeting was fixed from the outset: one of James's archbishops had made sure that the hall was crammed with orthodox Anglicans, and the few reformists were confined to an antechamber for several days, to show the King's displeasure. When finally they were admitted, James asked them what they sought. They replied, in the most conciliatory of terms, that their basic request was for freedom of conscience.

"I will none of that!", James shouted in reply.

Understandably daunted, the reformers made their last, almost pitifully modest request: that ministers no longer be obliged to wear surplices when leading Sunday services. James was livid: "Away with all your snivelling!", he shouted, before launching into a tirade that sounded all but indistinguishable from a declaration of war:

"I will *make* them conform, or I will harry them out of the land!"

James adopted the strict rules he had inherited from Elizabeth and made them stricter still. All private religious meetings were to be suppressed; the Book of Common Prayer was to be used at all services; and attendance by all subjects at an Anglican Communion at least three times a year was compulsory.

There were other disappointments. The more optimistic of the reformers had hoped that James would agree to limit the power of his Bishops. Again, he would have none of this. As for the Catholics ... their frustration with the King soon grew to murderous intensity, and reached its climax in the thwarted attempt to blow up both James and his House of Commons in the so-called Gunpowder Plot of 1605. To this day, the people of the United Kingdom still mark the event by setting off fireworks and burning effigies of the terrorist leader, Guido Fawkes, on the 5 November: "Guy Fawkes's Night".

So much for the broader sea of English history in the years leading up to *Mayflower*'s transatlantic adventure. In the country's backwaters, all but unnoticed by anyone in the capital, a great venture was being conceived.

Chapter Three

October 1620: The Men of the Voyage

For the Saints and Strangers, the experience of crossing the Atlantic might well be summed up in just four words:

First boredom, then fear.

Captain Christopher Jones

The voyagers intended destination was the mouth of the Hudson River, at that time part of the sprawling English possession known as Virginia, in honour of the Virgin Queen, Elizabeth.

Their captain, Mr Christopher Jones, was a highly experienced mariner. At fifty, he was one of the oldest men on board, and certainly one of the most skilled in all the arts of seamanship – he had been working on ships since early boyhood, and had been a Master of several vessels before *Mayflower*. The Pilgrims could hardly have chosen a better man: his temperament was cautious, but determined. He was a man of quiet courage, and he served them well.

By 1620, there were two main routes across the Atlantic. The longer, southern route was considered by far the safer – in fact, it could actually be a pleasant journey if the winds were fair. It involved meeting the trade winds, riding them south as far as the Azores, then steering west. The only real hazard was just off the coast of Spain – Finisterre, a peninsula stretching out from the west coast of Galicia. So many ships had been lost on the treacherous rocks that surrounded this peninsula that it became known as *Costa da Morte:* Death Coast.

The northern route was quicker. It meant sailing to the north and west in the general direction of Greenland, and then finding an Arctic current that would take the ships down towards the north-east coast of America. This was the route that intrepid English fishermen had been taking for about a century, and they shared their knowledge with other professional mariners.

Captain Jones opted to take the northern route, knowing full well that he was facing two additional challenges. For one thing, those English fishermen had always sailed in fine weather: across in spring, back at the end of summer. For another, the fisherman usually voyaged only as far as the Grand Banks. And Jones needed to make it all the way down the New England coast.

Captain Bartholomew Gosnold

Only one English captain had made the northern crossing to New England: Bartholomew Gosnold, who had sailed on *Concord* in 1603 as the leader of an expedition to New England authorised by Sir Walter Raleigh and organised by Sir Ferdinando Gorges – the man who, though he never set foot in America, did more than anyone to foster English colonies there.

Gosnold had covered himself with glory on the journey over, which he completed in just fifty largely trouble-free days – "not a man sick two days together". And he crowned his triumph by bringing the ship in to its exact destination in Massachusetts Bay, having rounded a headland which Gosnold named Cape Cod.

The success of Gosnold's venture gave an enormous boost to English dreams of new world colonies. He made a great deal of money selling furs and sassafras in London: rumour spread like a forest fire that a tea made from sassafras was a powerful cure-all. But Gosnold impressed Londoners even more with his tales of friendly and well-mannered Indians, some of whom had already picked up a few English words. The Indians, he said, liked everything about the English except their hot mustard, which made them pull funny faces in disgust. Moreover, they were eager to trade with Englishmen. And as for the New England soil, it was almost supernaturally fertile.

But to Captain Jones, what mattered most was not so much Gosnold's wealth as the fact that he had proved that the northern passage to New England could be done in safety, and in just fifty days. He was also more soberly aware that Gosnold had travelled in the summer. Fifty days…. With luck, or God, on their side, they might just make landfall before October was out.

Keeping a Course

The art of seamanship, as practised by Jones and his contemporaries, fell into two disciplines: pilotage and navigation. Pilotage was the science or craft of hugging the shore, which involved using charts (fairly elaborate and accurate by 1620) and pilotage books in conjunction with soundings. It was essential to take soundings, especially when visibility was reduced by rain and fog, to steer a ship through the exceptionally treacherous waters off the western coast of Europe.

Soundings were made by having a team of crew members pay out a long line, weighted with a lead. These were usually about 1,200 feet long, or 200 fathoms, with knots at regular intervals of six feet, a fathom. The sailors arranged the line along the length of the deck, until it ceased to uncoil, at which point a sailor would shout out either the number of fathoms plumbed or "no bottom". The result would be noted at noon every day.

Navigation called on a different set of skills. Sailing in deep water was relatively safe – no rocks to hit – but it meant crossing more or less uncharted waters with few useful instruments. Junior sailors or cabin boys were given the important duty of turning the ship's sand-glasses every half-hour: easy enough in calm waters, difficult when the ship was rolling wildly.

Lines could be used to estimate speed as well as depth: in fair weather, the same knotted line could be thrown overboard from the stern, and the Captain could see how rapidly the knots went over the side. This is, of course, the origin of the term "knot" as a unit of speed at sea.

The captain and his pilot had four other resources: the astrolabe, the quadrant, the traverse board and the compass. The astrolabe, a device of some antiquity (the mediaeval English poet Geoffey Chaucer had written a treatise on it for his son more than two hundred years earlier), was a reliable guide to the stars by which a ship could steer when the night skies were free from cloud. The quadrant, which had a sight for finding stars and a plumb-line hanging across a scale, could give a reasonably accurate reading of the latitude, provided the ship was sailing steadily.

The traverse board was used to estimate the course the ship was holding, or failing to hold. It took the form of a compass rose, and was pierced with holes in which a sailor would insert a small peg every half hour to record which direction the needle had been pointing. Once every four hours, the results would be tallied and passed on to the Captain. Given that the ship would travel an average of three miles an hour in good weather, the Captain could make an estimate of how far they had travelled as well as the direction of travel.

There were two main compasses, each balanced on a brass gimbal to keep it steady, and each lit by a lamp. The needles of these compasses had to be freshly magnetized from time to time by being rubbed with a lodestone.

All of these technological details we know from a variety of sources. But for events which took place on board, we have only one direct source. He was not trained as a historian, but in many ways he taught himself to be a very good one. And like the classical historian Thucydides, or the twentieth-century historian Winston Churchill, he had one great advantage on his side: he played a major part in the history he related. He was William Bradford, the devout, fragile boy of Scrooby.

Mr William Bradford

William Bradford was born on 19 March 1589. Though he was respected for his piety, diligence and evident intelligence as a young man, he did not show many signs of leadership or force of character until the hardships of colonial life brought out those latent virtues.

His short life had been full of sadness. Bradford's father had died the year after he was born; three years later his mother remarried, and William was sent to live with his grandfather. But his grandfather died in 1596, and his mother in 1597. He was adopted by his paternal uncles who began to train him for a life of farming. But Bradford had begun to ponder scripture deeply, and by the age of twelve he was making the long walk from his home in the village of Austerfield to join Clyfton's congregation in Babworth, to the objections of his family and the jeers of his neighbours.

This took great moral fibre. Luckily for young William, his lonely pilgrimage would soon be over. William Brewster took a shine to this eccentric, unworldly lad and became, in effect, the boy's father.

By now, King James's crack-down on secessionist Christians was at its most intense. Bradford fled to the Low Countries with the other Scrooby Separatists, lodging at first with his friends the Brewsters, and found employment as a weaver. In 1613 he took out Dutch citizenship papers, and a year later married a young English girl, Dorothy May. He also sold his modest plot of land in Austerfield and bought a house on the Achtergracht, or Back Canal. Here, Dorothy gave birth to their son, named John, probably in honour of John Robinson.

Crisis

During one exceptionally heavy storm, a main beam of *Mayflower* began to creak and buckle under the force of the mountainous waves. Eventually, it cracked.

At this point, the voyage could easily have come to an end. Some of the crew were convinced that this blow had weakened the ship to the point where she was no longer fit to complete the voyage: the best thing would be to turn back to England at once. The passengers, understandably alarmed by these ominous words, demanded that Jones and his officers deliver a verdict.

Jones – perhaps more courageous than prudent at this point – was insistent that *Mayflower* was still seaworthy. Though the upper portions of the ship could not be rendered sufficiently waterproof for the comfort of the wretched men, women and children below, there was, he insisted, no danger that she would take on so much water that she would be dragged down to the sea-bed. He was for sailing on. Anyway, he pointed out, they were by now much closer to the New World than the Old.

What helped Jones's view carry the day among the Pilgrims was an ingenious piece of repair work. Among the few pieces of relatively advanced technology brought along on the mission was an "iron jack screw" – probably intended for use in the Colony's printing press, for they had every intention of publishing their own books.

The ship's carpenter and his team managed to use this screw jack to raise the beam back into place so that it could be temporarily braced with a wooden post – "firm in the lower deck and otherwise bound." It had been a frightening episode, but Jones was resolute. And for their part, the sailors had for the first time on the journey been impressed by the Pilgrims' practical skill.

Chapter Four

Separatists in Holland: 1608 – 1620

In recent years, the people of the Low Countries had staged a remarkably successful rebellion against their Spanish enemy. The Seven Provinces of the Netherlands – Holland, Zeeland, Utrecht, Guelders, Friesland, Overijssel and Groningen – united in 1579 and then, in 1581, declared themselves a Republic.

This new Republic was to be governed by a shrewd compromise between modern parliamentary democracy and traditional monarchy. One principle enshrined in their new laws was that of religious toleration. Every citizen should "remain free in his religion, and no man be molested or questioned on the subject of Divine worship." The Separatists, watching with interest from England, understood this declaration to mean that what the Republic had really done was defy the Great Satan of Rome, and throw open their doors to their brothers and sisters in Protestantism.

In 1608, Robinson led his followers to Holland: first to

Amsterdam and then, about a year later, to Leyden, just a few miles north of The Hague and widely considered to be the most beautiful city in the Low Countries.

There were almost 500 of them, and at first they settled in well. They found a common place of worship in St Peter's Church, the Pieterskerk, and made their homes in a small group of streets clustered around this large and imposing House of God. The local economy was booming when they first arrived, and it was not hard for them to find employment, especially in the cloth industry for which Leyden was famous. Those who did not work in cloth set up small businesses of their own, often in the related trades, as tailors, glovers, milliners, and workers in silk.

But in political and religious terms, the most significant of their trades was publishing. Before long, the Separatists were turning out pamphlets in English, and having them smuggled across the water to their homeland.

For almost a decade, the Leyden community lived in quiet, hard-working contentment. They no longer dissented much among themselves, their businesses did well, and they earned the respect of their neighbours with their thrifty ways and complete honesty. Dutch employers were more than happy to employ these quiet English folk, confident that they would never be swindled or bilked.

But this peaceful time could not last. Back in March 1609, the United Provinces and Spain had signed a twelve-year peace treaty. That treaty was, thus, due to run out in 1621 – just a couple of years away. Perhaps it would be re-negotiated. More likely, or so the anxious Separatists feared, it would be the occasion for Spain to re-assert her former authority, wage a new war on the Republic and pull the tolerant nation back into the power of the Catholic Church. Which was to say: Satan.

They had other reasons for disquiet. A kind of generation gap, as we would now call it, had opened between old and young in their community. A regime of hard work and frugal diets had aged the adults prematurely, and they seemed to be growing weaker and more vulnerable to illness with each passing year.

More alarming still was the conduct of the rising generation. The young sons and daughters of the Separatists looked at the happier ways of their Dutch contemporaries and were openly envious. The sober English souls feared that their children were losing their English identity and were becoming more and more like their Dutch contemporaries, prey to "the great licentiousness of youth in that country and the manifold temptations of the place."

Some youngsters had already voted with their feet, and joined the Republic's army in search of a more exciting life. A few went back to England; others set off on more exotic travels around Europe. Separatist numbers were dwindling, and were not being made up by converts among the Dutch, who may have admired the reliability of their austere neighbours but had no intention of adopting their gloomy ways.

It was Robinson who proposed the dramatic solution: migrate to the New World.

At once, the Leyden community fell back into their old habit of arguing amongst themselves. They debated long and hard about the wisdom of this bold proposal. Those against it had powerful arguments on their side. Quite apart from the known perils of the long sea journey, there were the unknown dangers awaiting them on the far side.

But those in favour of the move were robust, above all

in their faith in a God who would never let down His elect. The "Indians" might indeed prove dangerous, but at least they were not Catholic; whereas the Spanish were both creatures of the Pope, and (so it seemed to the Separatists) obviously bent on the destruction of Protestants. Above all, there was the question of duty. The Gospel must be propagated in new lands.

The tide of opinion began to turn in favour of the would-be colonisers, and the Leyden elect began to talk seriously of America. But where should they go? Many favoured Guiana, the fabled home of the City of Gold, and the land to which Sir Walter Raleigh had sailed on his final, doomed adventure. The Dutch, eager to build up their own colonial possession of New Amsterdam – the city that would later be renamed New York – made a generous offer to fund the westward journey. The Separatists politely declined.

Their eyes turned to Virginia. The existing English settlement at Jamestown was out of the question: its inhabitants were deeply loyal to King James and his Church. But Northern Virginia, so far uncultivated by Europeans, was a more promising destination altogether. The Leyden elders drew up a formal proposal for the terms of their mission, emphasising their own loyalty to King James. Thus armed with an eminently reasonable document, they sent two of their best men to London to negotiate with the Virginia Company.

These men were John Carver, a successful merchant, and Robert Cushman. At first, their mission seemed promising. The Virginia Company assured them that the King would look kindly on their application. And, sure enough, James initially proved keen to support the idea, and gave his hearty consent to their cannily phrased appeal to enjoy liberty of conscience under his gracious protection. But it can hardly be doubted that he remembered those treasonable pamphlets from the Leyden press.

It should have been plain sailing from here on, but from this point the complications, setbacks and frustrations set in. Soon, Cushman was gloomily writing back to Leyden about all the squabbles that were taking place within the Virginia Company. Instead of working towards the great venture, the Company was wasting all its energies on in-fighting.

Then came discouraging news of a different kind. Another group of Leyden Separatists, 180 strong and led by a man named Francis Blackwell, had decided to set off for America on their own initiative, without bothering to secure a Patent. It was a murky affair, involving police raids, false confessions and perjured oaths. Blackwell managed to disentangle himself and travelled to the port of Gravesend, where he provisioned a ship and recruited a flock of faithful souls. They had been crammed "like herrings" into far too small a vessel.

The fresh water soon ran out; the ship was blown too far southwards; an epidemic of dysentery broke out below deck and soon 130 of the company were dead, including the master, six of his crew and Blackwell himself. A scratch crew of invalids and amateurs, now just 50 strong, finally brought the ship into Jamestown. This was such frightening news that many of the Leyden group decided that the perils of the sea were too great, and they resolved to stay in Holland.

Eventually, the squabbles inside the Virginia Company were more or less resolved and the promised Patent was issued on 9 June 1619. A copy was sent to Leyden so that the faithful could decide how best to act on it. Many of the congregation wanted to take the journey, but there was not enough money to send more than two ships in the first instance, so families would have to wait their turn.

Other difficulties now emerged. One of the thorniest issues involved the question of houses. The proposed contract, which was to run for seven years, determined that the company would support the colonisers throughout. At the end of the seven years, all profits would be divided equally between the Company and the colonists. But the colonists thought this inequitable and insisted that all the houses and other structures built by their labours should remain theirs and theirs alone.

Their objections did not go down well in London. One of the backers promptly withdrew his £500 stake. Others threatened to follow suit. If a compromise were not reached, the whole venture would founder. In the end, it seems, all sides tacitly agreed to go ahead with the voyage without the question of house rights being settled, with most parties probably reflecting that it was the least of the problems they collectively faced.

It was about now that others – the "Strangers", as they came to be known – were recruited by the Company, though they would not meet their counterparts until the eve of departure.

Cushman calculated the basic finances of the trip, and he delegated the buying of provisions to an Essex man, Christopher Martin. The epic Atlantic crossing would be done by two ships: a smaller one, which would bring the Leyden contingent to England, and a much larger vessel. The name of the small ship was *Speedwell*, and it was widely agreed that she would be an invaluable asset for a young colony.

Speedwell was at anchor in Delftshaven, not far from Rotterdam. After a special day of prayer, the 66 members of the Leyden congregation who had been selected for the trip set off for Delftshaven accompanied by families and well-wishers.

Though Robinson was the one who had first mooted the idea of emigration to America, he would remain in Leyden to care for the souls of those who were left behind. In Bradford's famous words:

> "With mutual embraces and many tears,
> they took their leaves one of another,
> which proved to be the last leave to many
> of them ... So they left that good and
> pleasant city which had been their resting
> place near twelve years: but they knew
> they were pilgrims, and looked not much
> upon these things, but lift up their eyes
> to the heavens, their dearest country, and
> quieted their hearts."

Bradford was the first writer to call the Separatists "pilgrims". It was not the name they generally gave themselves, and it did not really gain currency until well into the nineteenth century, but now the word has almost completely eclipsed "Separatists". So, from here on, let them be "Pilgrims".

The captain of *Speedwell* declared that it was time to sail. For once it was a pleasant journey and they reached their destination on the south coast of England in no more than three days. *Speedwell* spent a night at anchor in Southampton water, and on the following morning, 26 July 1620, pulled into the West Quay of Southampton itself. Just down the dock from them, the Pilgrims could see a larger ship, swarming with men who were loading her hulls with provisions.

Mayflower.

Chapter Five

Summer 1620: Enter the Strangers

Stephen Hopkins

"The stranger that dwelleth with you shall be as one of yourselves, and thou shalt love him as thyself."

Thomas Weston, the major investor in the *Mayflower* venture, was alarmed. He had learned that the number of Separatists prepared to take the great risk had begun to dwindle. Some had been frightened off by news of the recent catastrophic passage to America. Others found themselves reluctant to pay the price of the King's official sanction for their journey – that is, to play hypocrite and pass themselves off as observing Anglicans as well as loyal subjects.

And some were simply reluctant to expose their children to the dangers and hardships. Bradford summed it up ruefully: "And thus this small number was divided, as if the Lord thought these few too many for the great work he had to do."

Weston trusted in himself rather than the Lord. He took immediate and decisive action. Over seventy Merchant Adventurers had agreed to back his enterprise, and if there were too few passengers to make the journey practicable, his hopes of making a handsome profit would be dashed. So he set about recruiting others who might be willing to make the hazardous trip, no matter what their religious views.

Most of these "Strangers", as they came to be called (after a passage from scripture that the Saints quoted a good deal at this time), were from Essex and London and Kent. The first man Weston approached was one who enjoyed the rare distinction of already having made the journey to America, and who was familiar with the ways of the "salvages" there: Mr Stephen Hopkins.

Hopkins' imagination had been fired by the recent visit to England of the American princess Pocohontas, who had married an Englishman named John Rolfe, and had been baptized into the Anglican church with the Old Testament name Rebecca. Her visit to England proved to be a wonder of the age, and it was said that her presence inspired more English folk to dream of the New World's glories than all of the written propaganda for colonial expansion put together.

Hopkins came from a remote part of the Cotswolds, near Wootton-Under-Edge, in Gloucestershire. He was born on 29 October 1581, which made him almost forty when he joined forces with the Saints. His first great voyage had been on *Sea Venture*, in 1609. A terrifying storm had scattered the flotilla, and *Sea Venture* was washed up in Bermuda – a place which, to the amazement of all, proved to be a kind of earthly paradise.

Bermuda was beautiful, and warm, and sweetly scented, with the delightful song of tropical birds filling the air. The seas yielded an abundance of cod, mullet, pilchards, bonito and shark. The land was full of easily captured beasts, including tortoises (delicious roasted) and hogs.

Some of the sailors began to reflect that, in this holiday world, there was no distinction between master and man. Why push on to Jamestown, where the masters lived in idle luxury and the men were all but slaves? Why not set up a colony of their own? Hopkins saw the force of these mutinous words, and he argued eloquently that the men should no longer recognise the authority of their leaders. The leaders, in turn, had him handcuffed.

Hopkins was threatened with the death penalty, but he pleaded his case with eloquence. Almost everybody thought he was a thoroughly likeable man, so he was fully pardoned. Eventually, the company built two new ships from the timber of *Sea Venture*, and made their way to Jamestown.

Hopkins returned to London in the last days of 1609 to find that his wife had recently died after giving birth to a son christened Stephen, who had also died. He was distraught and guilt-ridden; fortunately, his successful brother Robert offered to shelter him and his two surviving children in his comfortable house.

Hopkins now embarked on a new life in the weaving trade. He moved to a house outside the London wall. Just down the road was Heneage House, a well-known "nest of non-conformists". There had been clandestine Separatists in Whitechapel since 1571, many of them in the weaving trade.

It was at Heneage House, in 1617, that Stephen Hopkins met some names that will be familiar by now:

John Carver and Robert Cushman, over from Holland; and William Brewster – all three of them members of John Robinson's congregation. Brewster had been chosen by Robinson as the man who would be their next minister, in America, should he and the others survive.

There was one other incentive for emigration. London's old enemy, plague, had broken out again, and Hopkins believed that his family would live more healthily under cleaner skies. He would bring with him his heavily pregnant second wife Elizabeth, *née* Fisher, and his three children – Constance, now 15, Giles 13; and the infant Daris – as well as two indentured servants, Edward Dotey and Edward Leister. The Hopkinses were the largest single family group of London Strangers.

Rendezvous at Southampton

From our perspective, the most colourful of the Strangers was Miles Standish, who came from a Catholic family. Short, red-haired and quick-tempered, Standish had been trained as a soldier in the Low Countries, where he had also met and become firm friends with John Robinson.

Standish was, like Hopkins, one of the senior members of the party: he was just three years younger than Hopkins, and they, too, became lifelong friends. They actually looked like brothers, since Hopkins was also red-haired and short of stature. When Standish found out that had Hopkins had in his younger days served with the local militia at Wootton-Under-Edge, he appointed the Whitechapel merchant as his right-hand man.

One of the things that united these two practical and worldly-wise men was their dismay when they discovered, in Southampton, just how ill-prepared many of the Saints were for life in the New World. They continued to insist that they would support themselves by fishing, but they had little experience as fishermen, and had brought along highly unsuitable gear. They said that they intended to trade with the natives, but knew next to nothing of the Native Americans' language or culture, and had not brought very much with which to trade. Nor had they brought many muskets, or much armour.

On Wednesday, 26 July, a fine day, *Speedwell* reached her appointed anchorage at the mouth of the Test river near the West Quay at Southampton. Nearby was another ship, about three times larger than *Speedwell*, its decks busy with men loading cargo. *Speedwell* dropped her anchor next to *Mayflower*. The Saints and the Strangers met on the Quay, and greeted each other heartily and with goodwill. Unfortunately, this cheerful mood did not prevail for long.

Mayflower

There were many ships called *Mayflower*; a ship of that name had taken part in the English retaliation against the Spanish Armada. The *Mayflower* in dock at Southampton was probably that which is first listed in the port records of London in 1606, when the master was one Robert Bonner, of Leigh.

Mayflower had been used mainly in the wine trade –

that is to say, to export goods (mainly cloth and animal skins) from England to La Rochelle and Bordeaux, and to import French wines and brandies back to London. She had also sailed to Norway and Hamburg. Her most recently recorded voyage of 1620 had been a run to La Rochelle and back on 23 May. About three weeks later, Weston and Robert Cushman chartered her for an Atlantic trip. So *Mayflower*, used to hugging the shores of England and the Continent, would also be sailing in unfamiliar waters

Almost all of the food – apart from some cheeses, salt, and "strong waters" from Leyden – had to be bought from the butchers, bakers and grocers of Southampton. Most of the fish and meat was preserved rather than fresh: plenty of dried salt cod (known as "haberdyne"), dried ox tongues (known as "neats' tongues"), salted beef and pork; smoked herrings, smoked pork and beef; spiced meats and pickled eggs. For vegetables they had cabbages, onions, beans, parsnips, turnips, peas (and "pease pudding"). There were firkins of butter, as well as plenty of oatmeal, rye meal and wheat flour.

Then there were the all-important spices: long valued in England for their use in preserving perishable foodstuffs and adding a degree of variety to a limited diet especially in the winter months: pepper, ginger, cinnamon, mace, nutmeg. There were jams and other sweet preserves, dried fruits including currants and raisins and prunes. And, of course, there were abundant quantities of wine and beer.

There were also animals on board: no horses, cows, oxen or donkeys, but some sheep, pigs, goats and fowls, all intended to be kept alive and well for their prosperous future on the farms the Pilgrims hoped to set up in the

New World. These were kept forward, on the spar deck; a few other, smaller animals, such as rabbits, were kept in the boats as a potential source of fresh meat. And some of those on board had brought their pets along: Peter Browne was accompanied by his mastiff, and John Goodman by his spaniel. Many of the Pilgrims brought along cage birds.

They took books, too – mostly Bibles and religious tracts, including Robinson's *Justification of Separation* (1610), in the possession of Bradford and signed by the author. There were also agricultural textbooks, almanacs, hornbooks for the children, and calendars. Dr Fuller took a few medical books (though most of his personal library was theological), while Standish combined books of military lore (Caesar's *Commentaries*, Bariffe's *Artillery*) with more general learning – a history of the world and, for some reason, a history of Turkey.

Captain Jones and his Crew

Jones had between twenty to thirty crew members for the journey, including John Clare, the pilot; Robert Coppin – second mate; Andrew Williamson – ship's merchant [that is, purser]; John Parker; Giles Heale – a young man trained as a Barber-Surgeon; John Parker; Thomas (?) Jones; and a Mr Leaver [first name not recorded]. There were also men we know only by their jobs: a carpenter; a bosun [boatswain: the man in charge of the rigging, and of training younger sailors in the art of knots]; a gunner; four quartermasters; and a cook.

False Starts, Monetary Woes and Delays

After the initial happy meeting of Strangers and Saints, the arguing began. Among the most pressing worries was money. Weston had run up debts that needed to be settled before the two ships could sail. Many angry words later, he threatened to pull out of the deal.

Realising that they had little alternative, the Leyden group resolved to raise money to clear their debts in a potentially risky way. They sold a large part of their supply of butter (according to Bradford's account, between 3360 and 4720 pounds of it) and various other provisions, and paid off what they owed.

It was not until 8 August that the two ships finally put to sea. Within days, they were in trouble. The winds had turned against them – not to a degree that might be threatening but enough to make her progress sluggish. More worrying to Captain Reynolds of *Speedwell* was that she was seriously over-masted for her size – meaning that the weight of sail she was carrying was so great as to risk dragging her under. Moreover, she was leaking quite badly. Reynolds signalled to *Mayflower* that she should come alongside. He conferred with Jones, who reluctantly agreed that they should go ashore for repairs. The winds still against them, they made their way to Dartmouth, where they stayed for more than a week.

There were problems of shipboard discipline and morale, too. Robert Cushman wrote a painful letter to his friend Edward Southwark, at Heneage House, describing these difficult days:

Besides the eminent dangers of this voyage, which are no less than deadly, an infirmity of body hath seized me, which will not in all likelihood leave me till death ... Our pinnace [the *Speedwell*], will not cease leaking ... We put in here to trim her and I think that if we had stayed at sea but three or four hours more, she would have sunk right down ... Our victuals will be half eaten up, I fear, before we go from the coast of England....

Friend, if ever we make a plantation, God works a miracle ...

Finally, they were ready to try again.

The Fate of Speedwell

On Wednesday, 23 August, the two ships set sail again.

When she was well to the west of Land's End, *Speedwell* was once again leaking to a dangerous degree. Jones gave his ruling – they would turn back and put into dock at Plymouth. Had they not made this crucial detour, their New World settlement might easily have been named Southampton Plantation. They stayed in Plymouth for a further ten days.

When she was examined, *Speedwell* was found not to have one or two major holes in her structure, but rather to be riddled with countless much smaller holes. The verdict was inescapable. "She would not prove sufficient for the voyage" and would have to be abandoned. Some of her passengers and most of her stores were transferred to the already crowded *Mayflower*; others, by now thoroughly disheartened, decided to give up altogether. About twenty people left the mission at this point, including the invalid Robert Cushman and his family.

Every day they spent in Plymouth added to the danger. Their supplies were dwindling, and the weather was on the turn. Within a matter of days it would be time for the first autumn storms. Only one previous expedition had sailed the northern route from the old England to the new England, and that crossing had been made in summer. Perhaps it was already too late to have any hope of a trouble-free journey.

Just before their true and final departure, Sir Ferdinando Gorges treated the leaders of the group to a handsome dinner at his house on Plymouth Hoe. Edward Winslow recalled:

> Wednesday, the sixth of September, the wind coming east-north-west, a fine small gale, we loosed from England, having been kindly entertained and courteously used by divers friends there dwelling ...

It was the last good meal they would enjoy for over a year.

Chapter Six

November and December 1620: Landfall

Towards the last days of October, the equinoctial storms finally began to ease. The omens were mixed: a birth, a death.

Elizabeth Hopkins, wife of Stephen, gave birth to a son. Her labour would have been more than the usual ordeal undergone by Jacobean women, since it took place in freezing, dark, wet and filthy conditions – there were no lying-in sheets, indeed there was hardly any clean or dry linen of any kind. She was "creamped" up in the small dark space of her improvised cabin, no bigger than the average sheep stall on an English farm. There were two trained doctors on board: Samuel Fuller, a Leyden saint, and the aptly named Giles Heale, a crew member; but attending childbirth was women's work.

When her agony was finally done, she held the newborn boy-child in her arms and asked the women who had seen her through her confinement to open a small, sealed box she had kept safe for this event. In it they found dry baby clothes and a thick, dry blanket. Without this foresight, the poor infant might easily have died of cold before *Mayflower* landed. Captain Jones, who had the traditional privilege of being allowed to perform at sea the offices reserved for ministers on land, presided at the christening and gave the boy his name: Oceanus.

The death came a few days later: young William Button of Austerfield, a servant of Samuel Fuller, died of an unidentified illness. His body was cast into the sea on Tuesday, 7 November. He was the only passenger to die on the crossing.

The grimness of Button's funeral ceremony was tempered by signs that the voyagers' ordeal might soon be over. Sharp-eyed crewmen noted bits and pieces of driftwood in the waters lapping around the hull. The wind began to drop, and the passengers sank into exhausted sleep. In the lull, the cries of birds could be heard overhead. Land birds. Jones ordered his men to start taking soundings again, and discovered that the coastal shelf below them was rising. This final calm of the voyage – half ominous, half optimistic – lasted for two more days after Button's funeral. On the morning of the third day, Friday, 10 November, the lookout shouted "Land ho!"

Passengers dragged themselves from their damp, cold bedding and clambered up on deck. Ahead of them in the chill morning mist was what Captain Jones believed – correctly – to be Cape Cod. *Mayflower* had made landfall much too far to the North. No matter – land was land, and they were heartened and relieved to see it. Or, in Bradford's charmingly understated phrase: "They were not a little joyful …"

Jones fell into hurried discussions with Carver and

others. They soon decided not to yield to the obvious temptation and rush ashore at once, but to carry out the mission as planned. So, the weather now being fine and the winds favourable, Jones turned *Mayflower* to the south and set sail down the coast towards their intended destination, the Hudson River.

Not for long, though. After just a few hours under sail, she hit dangerous waters in an area near Monomoy Island now known as Pollock Rip. Jones persisted in his southerly course for a short while longer and then, to the relief of his passengers, went for the safer option and, as night came on, turned north again towards Cape Cod.

Mayflower sailed through the night. By the time the sun was up, she was back at the Cape, in the calm waters within its northern hook. The crew hauled down the sails; the anchor was dropped. They had done it. And the more thoughtful among them knew that they had accomplished something remarkable. Bradford, recalling the moment many years later, was moved to exceptional eloquence. It is one of the great moments of his narrative:

> But here I cannot but stay and make a
> pause, and stand half amazed at this poor
> people's present condition; and so I
> think will the reader, too, when he well
> considers the same ...
>
> Besides, what could they see but a hideous
> and desolate wilderness, full of wild beasts
> and wild men – and what multitudes
> of them there might be they knew not.
> Neither could they, as it were, go up

to the top of Pisgah to view from this
wilderness a more goodly country to feed
their hopes; for which way soever they
turned their eyes (save upward to the
heavens) they could have little solace or
content in respect of any outward objects.
For summer being done, all things stand
upon them with a weather-beaten face,
and the whole country, full of woods and
thickets, represented a wild and savage hue.

It was not yet time to row ashore. First, there were principles to settle.

The Mayflower Compact.

It had already dawned on most of the passengers that they
had landed in a territory well to the north of the land they
had contracted to settle: that they were, in other words,
about to venture onto land to which they had no legal
right, and in which there were as yet no English laws.
Some of the Strangers were talking in threatening terms
about their intention to act as they saw fit.

The leaders acted swiftly and decisively. They drew up a
document, and called a general meeting in the great cabin
at which each head of family, and a few other single men
of adult age, was given a pen and instructed to sign. Forty-
one men signed.

It began by asserting first their piety and next their
enduring loyalty to their King (or, at any rate, their will-

ingness to go along with a necessary legal requirement to state such loyalty)

In the Name of God, Amen.

> We whose names are underwritten, the
> loyal subjects of our dread sovereign
> Lord, King James, by the Grace of God,
> of Great Britain, France and Ireland,
> defender of the faith, etc....

John Carver, the first man to sign, was elected as first governor.

The *Mayflower* Compact has long been the subject of heated debate. Some believe that it was the founding statement of democratic principle in what would eventually become the United States. Others point out that the most urgent point of the document was not to safeguard democratic "liberty", but to put strict limits on the potentially dangerous liberty that some of the Strangers desired.

Ashore

Sixteen men launched the *Mayflower*'s longboat and went to see what the land might offer or threaten. They brought back mixed reports: no obvious enemies, or ferocious creatures; not much in the way of fresh water; but plenty of useful trees and plants, including sassafras and juniper, and "spit's deep excellent black earth" which boded well for farming next year. The others began to unload, and to shuttle to and fro between *Mayflower* and land.

On Monday, 13 November 1620, work on establishing the colony began in earnest.

Apart from the sheer joy of being able once again to stand upright on an unmoving earth, one of the first pleasures they knew was cleanliness and the warmth of bonfires. Women took their filthy garments and sheets ashore and began to wash them in a nearby still pond – its waters a little stagnant and unpleasant to taste, but at least not seawater. For the first time in two months they all could breathe sweet, fresh air instead of the mephitic stench from *Mayflower*'s lower depths.

While the women began to restore a degree of comfort, the men went about other kinds of business. Some scavenged around on the beaches, where they found an abundance of cherrystones and other clams, the kinds that are a famous local delicacy to this day. Starved of fresh meat for weeks, now they gorged themselves … and made themselves thoroughly sick.

Other, more prudent men set to work hoisting the parts of the shallop from *Mayflower*'s main deck, and slowly re-assembling it on shore, making the necessary repairs as they went along. And a third set of men, 16 in all, set out on the morning of 15 November loaded with muskets to make a proper exploration of the surrounding country. The man chosen to lead this party was Captain Miles Standish.

Standish's party included William Bradford and John Carver; also Edward Winslow, John and Edward Tilley, Edward Doty and four of the *Mayflower* crew. They had hardly begun their explorations when they noticed that they were not alone in the wilderness. Five or six Native

Americans were wandering in their direction. These strangers stopped in surprise; huddled; and ran off into the woods. The Englishmen ran after them, not with evil intent but simply wishing to learn more of their surroundings, but this made the natives run all the faster, until their pursuers were quite lost.

The English camped overnight, and the following morning set off in search of the place where the natives might live. It was hard work beating through the thorns and bushes in their way, and thirsty work, too, as they could not find any water fit to drink. Finally, they came across a spring, and fell on it with relief: Bradford recalled that this water was "now in great thirst as pleasant unto them as wine or beer had been in foretimes." This place now bears the name Pilgrim Spring.

As they continued their survey, the explorers discovered human remains, lying alongside several arrows and a bow. A warrior's grave! They buried the bones and trappings with due solemnity. Their next discovery was more cheering – a place which must until recently have been a house and its gardens, as well as a large kettle and an ample quantity of corn, to which they helped themselves.

There was double cause for celebration that night: this windfall of corn, and another birth. Mistress Susana White had produced a baby son, the first of the colonists' children to be born on American soil. They christened him Peregrine: "pilgrim".

About a week and a half later, the shallop was finally ready to take to the waters. Captain Jones took charge of this two-day expedition, accompanied by thirty men. The weather was now growing more severe, and on their first night away from *Mayflower* the wind was intense. Six inches of snow fell in just a couple of hours. Some of the party decided that they would be better off on land, and waded ashore through the chilling waters – some of them, Bradford said, thereby catching colds that would soon prove fatal.

Their first major discovery was a brace of wigwams, in the style (as they would learn) of the Nauset people. But there was no sign of the Nauset themselves. The Nauset had heard of these strange new people in their land, and had retreated until they could work out whether the white men had come to trade or to massacre. Again, the explorers found a good quantity of corn in these wigwams – more than enough to have a surplus of seeds to plant in 1621. They returned to *Mayflower* triumphant.

Building

The winter was drawing in with frightening speed, and if they were not all to perish of cold, the colonists needed to start building.

A young boy's prank almost killed them all. Understandably restless after weeks of being cooped up in darkness, a fourteen-year old lad named Francis Billingham decided, like countless other boys across the centuries, to make himself some deliciously noisy fireworks – "squibs". His father's cabin contained an open barrel of gunpowder, its contents spilling onto the floor. Just four feet divided the bed from the barrel, and it was in this tiny space that Francis gleefully fired off three of his squibs. Was it Divine Intervention or just the omnipresent damp that prevented the gunpowder from exploding, and blowing *Mayflower* apart? In any event, no one was hurt, not even the foolhardy Francis.

First Encounter

A few days later, the newcomers finally had their first confrontation with the locals. A small party of explorers, who were using the shallop to investigate the coastline and the nearby forests, was suddenly fired upon with arrows. They retaliated with musket shots, and soon their assailants fled. True to their ways, the Pilgrims knelt on the ground and gave thanks to their Lord for having survived this skirmish. They named the site of their modest battle First Encounter.

They returned to the shallop and set off again in search of a good harbouring spot. The weather had once more turned very bad, and the small boat was being thrown around so severely that the rudder broke. The oarsmen had to pull with all their might to keep moving in the right direction. Then came near-disaster: their mast shattered and the sail fell overboard. Rowing for their lives through the darkness, the Pilgrims finally reached relative safety in the lee of a small island, where they sheltered until the next morning. They crawled ashore, numb with cold and wet, and built a fire to keep themselves alive. Finally, their luck improved. There were no hostile natives on this island, and the weather lifted: cold, but sunny and calm.

They spent all day Saturday drying themselves out, and all day Sunday observing the Sabbath. Then they re-boarded the shallop, and rowed along the shoreline until they found a spot that might suit *Mayflower*. They had reached the western side of Cape Cod Bay 45 miles from their landfall at what is now Wellfleet on the Cape's easternmost hook.

Plymouth Rock

Sixteen men stepped ashore and surveyed the area for its possibilities.

It was a strip of land between Captain's Hill, as they named it, and Plymouth Rock. They had to admit that it wasn't perfect. Most obviously, there was no great river leading off into the potential riches further inland. The soil was not as rich as that they had known in the eastern Cod, and the water in the harbour was not as deep as they might have wished, which meant that *Mayflower* would have to anchor slightly over a mile away. Still, it was passable. As Bradford said, they considered it

> A place (as they supposed) fit for the situation. At least it was the best they could find, and the season and their present necessity made them glad to accept of it.

And so they went back to *Mayflower* and told their shipmates that they had found the site of their future home.

On Saturday, 16 December 1620, *Mayflower* dropped anchor in Plymouth harbour. Bradford was stirred to unusual eloquence:

> May not and ought not the children of these
> fathers rightly say: our fathers were English-
> men which came over the great ocean, and
> were ready to perish in this wilderness.

Bradford's pride at this grand accomplishment was tempered by personal sorrow. When the shallop party returned from their reconnaissance, they were told that Dorothy Bradford, William's "dearest consort", had fallen overboard and drowned. Was this a genuine misadventure, or had she despaired of their desolate new land, and killed herself?

Soon, others would have their own cause for mourning.

All members of the *Mayflower* company had been weakened by their ordeals and, as the temperature plunged, many fell ill. As the last days of the last month of the momentous year grew shorter and shorter, one by one, the ill began to die.

Chapter Seven

1620 – 1621: *Misery and Miracles*

The first building the newcomers put up was a simple shed-like structure in which they stored the cargo that was being unloaded from *Mayflower* – a tricky and tiring chore, since the ship was anchored in deeper water about a mile and a half away, and the weather was bad: rain, sleet or snow almost every day. Next, twenty men, including Stephen Hopkins and his two servants, started work on a common dwelling house – no more than twenty feet by twenty feet, with a thatched roof in the familiar English style and a few small windows (made of oiled paper) to let some slivers of pale light penetrate the gloom.

Most of the settlers would live here through the first winter, in effect huddling together for warmth; others made themselves even more primitive shelters – small wooden huts with roofs of turf. But three days of storms set in, and the work had to cease; and though every able-bodied man with no other urgent task helped to cut timber, and saw and carry wood, the winds and rains thwarted their task again and again.

Just nine days after *Mayflower* dropped anchor, it was Christmas. The Pilgrims did not celebrate that date as a religious festival, but Captain Jones was a Church of England man, and he ordered his men to bring up one of the last precious barrels of beer so that Christmas on board ship, at least, should be merry in the old English way. Three days later, on 28 December, work began in earnest on constructing the houses that would make up the Pilgrims' town and the fort that might protect it. They drew up plans: to start with, there would be nineteen houses, one per major family group with single men as lodgers. The town, set on top of a hill high enough that they could see as far as Cape Cod on clear days, would be laid out in the shape of a cross, with one vertical and one horizontal street. A pious form to be sure, but also a practical one, as they considered that such a layout would be easy to defend against raiders.

It should have been a promising start, but the late season was against them. So was their poor health. Weakened and malnourished by the recent long journey, and unable to find the fresh fruits and vegetables that might otherwise have restored them, the people who had managed to stay alive at sea now grew sick on land. Those already suffering from scurvy easily caught severe colds; the colds soon worsened into pneumonia. Those still living on board *Mayflower* were anxious to move ashore as soon as they could because conditions on board were now so insanitary that it had become a kind of plague ship.

Six pilgrims had died by the turn of the New Year. Eight more perished in January, including Rose Standish who died in her cabin on 29 January – followed by another seventeen in February and thirteen in March.

Then, as if their bodily woes were not affliction enough, the Pilgrims suffered another potential catastrophic accident. On 14 January, the thatch of the common-house's still-incomplete roof caught fire. If sparks or flames were to come into contact with their generous stores of gunpowder, the whole building would be blown to pieces. The many sick and the few healthy joined forces in a frantic, panicked attempt to move the gunpowder barrels off to a safe distance. They succeeded, though they lost a good deal of their clothing and bedding to the flames.

It was all a dreadful, sickening ordeal, and yet it also served to bring out the best and most admirable qualities of the Pilgrims – not least those of Miles Standish and old man Brewster, who tended to both the worldly and the spiritual needs of his flock – working on the land, caring for the sick in their often filthy beds, and preaching words of encouragement every Sunday.

Bradford recalled these times in moving detail:

> In two or three months' time half of their
> company died, especially in January and
> February, being the depth of winter, and
> wanting houses and other comforts; being
> infected with the scurvy and other diseases
> which this long voyage had brought upon
> them, so there died sometimes two or
> three of a day. Of 100 and odd persons,
> scarce fifty remained. And of these, in the
> time of most distress, there was but six or
> seven sound persons who, to their great
> commendations be it spoken, spared no

pains night or day, but with abundance of
toil and hazard of their own health, fetched
them wood, made them fires, dressed
them meat, made their beds, washed their
loathsome clothes, clothed and unclothed
them. In a word, did all the homely and
necessary offices for them which dainty
and queasy stomachs cannot endure to hear
named; and all this willingly and cheerfully,
without any grudging in the least, showing
herein their true love unto their friends and
brethren; a rare example and worthy to be
recommended.

But these exemplary people were the former passengers:
the Saints. The professional sailors were by no means so
noble. When sickness broke out on board *Mayflower* at
anchor, the healthy sailors refused to risk their lives by
going down to care for their ailing shipmates, no matter
how much they had roistered together. The dying, they
said, should simply be left alone to die as quickly as possible. It fell to the Pilgrims still on board to care for the
dying mariners, and to their great credit they did so with
as much solicitude as they gave their own people.

Their dead were buried secretly, at night, at a nearby
site they named Coles Hill, in graves that were carefully
flattened so as not to draw attention. One of the graves
held the mortal remains of Mary Allerton, whose child
had been stillborn. Why all the secrecy? Because they did
not wish to give away their weakness to potential enemies.

At night-time, they could hear the noises of wild
animals in the forests and from time to time they saw

Native Americans, too. For the most part, these watchful figures would run away when spotted, but towards the end of February a party of some twelve natives raided a work site in the woods close to the plantation and stole some tools. Alarmed, the pilgrims resolved to protect themselves more vigorously, and appointed Miles Standish as their Captain-General. It was a position he would hold for the next forty years.

Their profound faith in God aside, the Pilgrims would have had every reason simply to despair. In fact, though they had no way of knowing this, they had by early March already passed through the worst of their ordeal. As the hours of sunlight grew longer with the approach of their first spring, those fit to work spent daylight hours sowing their first crop of peas and beans. The Hopkins family, who had brought over a good supply of seeds also planted carrots, cabbages, radishes and – for a touch of luxury – melons.

The weather grew milder, the warm wind came up from the south, and birds began to sing in the woods. Young Francis Billington, the fireworks enthusiast, made up for his earlier misdemeanor by discovering a large pond of fresh water, full of fish. The adults said that he might amount to something after all, if he could manage to escape the gallows, and named the pond Billington's Sea, the name it still has today.

Then something even more surprising happened. It bordered on the miraculous.

Samoset

One day, a single Native American man approached the plantation. He was tall, and dignified – "of seemly carriage" – and all but naked in the cold weather, wearing nothing but "a leather about his waist with a fringe about a span long or a little more." He had a clean-shaven face, and his black hair was worn short above his brows but fell down freely at the back over his neck and shoulders. He was armed, carrying a bow and two arrows, but as far as the residents could judge, he had not come to attack them. When he was within a few yards he stopped and addressed them. They were astonished. He spoke in English.

"Welcome!"

This extraordinary man went on to tell them that his name was Samoset, that he was a Sagamore, of the Algonquin nation, and that he had come from a territory to their north, more than a hundred miles from here: to be exact, from the Maine peninsula today known as Pemaquid Point. When Samoset was growing up in that region, he had often seen English ships fishing in the waters around Monhegan – only, he said, about five days' walk from Plymouth, or a single day's sail if the winds were fair. He had made friends with these fishermen, enjoyed the treats they gave him from their store of provisions, and had learned to speak a simple but serviceable form of English.

The Pilgrims dressed him up in a warm coat, and took him to Stephen Hopkins's unfinished house. Samoset, having acquired a taste for ales, asked them if he could have a drink of their beer. His hosts responded by plying him with a spread of what he took to be proper English food: some roast duck, corn pudding, cheese with ship's biscuits and butter, and "strong water" – in this case, brandy. It was a generous gesture from people who had to be cautious about their stores, but the information he gave them was more than handsome recompense.

Samoset explained the intricacies of local politics. The settlers, he assured them, need not be afraid of their nearby neighbours, who were essentially friendly and peaceable folk who had, anyway, four years earlier adopted the policy of staying out of "Patuxet" – their name for Plymouth – after a plague had killed an entire small community. This plague, though no one understood as much at the time, was almost certainly smallpox – a disease unwittingly brought over by Europeans, whose forebears had developed a measure of immunity. The natives had no such genetic defences.

Samoset went on with his explanations. The hostile natives who had attacked them and stolen their tools, he said, were the Nauset people, about a hundred strong. The Nauset had engaged in skirmishes with earlier English travellers. Nauset warriors had killed several of the English party. But the conduct of the English had hardly been blameless, either: one of them had taken twenty Patuxets and seven Nausets captive, and had shipped them to Spain where they were sold as slaves. (One of these slaves would soon play a significant part in the Pilgrim's story.)

Since Samoset was clearly enjoying his food and conversation, the Pilgrims thought it best to let him stay, and so they offered him space in Stephen Hopkins's modest hut. The following morning, they made him a present of a small knife, a bracelet and a ring. In return, he agreed to bring back fellow countrymen to begin trading. And after an abortive start – abortive largely because the first few potential traders came back with him on a Sunday, when no Pilgrim could do business – he was as good as his word.

Massasoit and Squanto

The first major act of Pilgrim diplomacy took place on 1 April, when Samoset returned with what amounted to an ambassadorial procession: some sixty natives, all male, all tall, and most with their faces painted in bold colours – red, yellow, black, white. Their leader, Massasoit, was an imposing man, taciturn and dignified, quite elaborately dressed in a deerskin, with a leather tobacco pouch, a knife, and beads. Massasoit's face was dyed mulberry.

It fell to Edward Winslow to be the Pilgrim's spokesman, and he did the job well, with due solemnity and sense of occasion. Winslow presented Massasoit with several pleasing gifts: knives, a ring, English food and a pot of "strong water". He assured Massasoit, through a new interpreter, that King James of England was anxious to make a peace treaty with his mighty people. This seems to have gone down well with the chief, who at once agreed to come into one of their houses to parley with the Pilgrim "chief", John Carver. The Pilgrims had little taste for drama, but they improvised a piece of theatrical pomp and circumstances including drums, trumpets and even some marching musketeers.

Carver and Massasoit bowed to each other; Carver kissed Massasoit's hand; Massasoit gave Carter a friendly bear hug. They sat down, and Carver called for roast meat and brandy. Massasoit, not knowing how strong European potations can be, coughed and spluttered and broke into a hot sweat. But he recovered enough dignity for the negotiations to proceed. It was a crucial treaty for the Pilgrims, and Massasoit and his heirs kept to it (for the most part) for the next half century and more. Both sides agreed to give each other full support in case of attack by other nations; to outlaw any acts of theft, and to live in peace. Massasoit also agreed to spread word of this treaty all around the region, and to send any of his people who might be caught in criminal acts against the newcomers to be tried and if need be punished in the Plantation.

The Pilgrims would reap other, incidental benefits from this momentous day. Samoset's English was a little too rudimentary for the complexities of political bargaining, so Massasoit had brought along another Native American who could not only speak English but could speak it fluently. This was Tisquantum, usually called "Squanto", who over the centuries has come to be probably the most famous Native American of his age. (The Disney company made a feature about him in 1994: *Squanto, A Warrior's Tale*). Squanto's life was one of far-flung adventures and misadventures.

Squanto had travelled to England in 1605 on a ship captained by one George Weymouth. After almost a decade, he travelled back to the New World on a voyage led by Captain John Smith. But one of Smith's junior officers was a villain: he managed to persuade Squanto and others to board his own ship, kidnapped them and sold them as slaves in Malaga. Fortunately for those kidnapped, some local friars took up their cause, had them freed, and brought them to live with their order with a view to converting them to the true God.

Evidently a quick and resourceful fellow, Squanto managed to persuade his rescuers that he belonged in England, and he made his way back to London where he found employment and lodgings with a ship-builder, John Slaney. When Slaney set out on an expedition of his own, to Newfoundland, he employed Squanto as a translator and guide. Soon after this, in 1619, Squanto joined an expedition along the New England coast. When he reached Patuxet, he found that all his people had died of the "plague" – the pilgrims had heard this story already, from Samoset. So, a man without living relatives, he joined Massasoit.

Despite his experiences of betrayal, Squanto devoted the rest of his life to helping the white folk survive in their new home. He showed them the local ways of fishing for eels and "menhaden", and of planting corn and using decayed fish bodies to fertilise the earth; he continued to interpret for them, and help them to explore the wilderness all about them. But his life was to be cut short. On the way back from a diplomatic mission to the Wampanoag people, he fell ill, and died on 30 November 1622. Bradford gives the details:

> Squanto fell ill of an Indian fever, bleeding much at the nose, which the Indians take as a symptom of death, and within a few days he died. He begged the Governor to pray for him, that he might go to the Englishman's God in Heaven, and bequeathed several of his things to his English friends, as remembrances. His death was a great loss.

As usual, Bradford understates the case. The Pilgrims would have had every justification to consider Squanto an agent sent by God to help them survive the rigours of this unforgiving land.

Counting the Cost

The spring came and the sick grew healthy again, though the warm months saw a few more deaths, including that of the Governor, John Carver, who suffered a stroke while digging in the fields, fell into a coma and died soon after. He had, his neighbours thought, simply worked himself to death. His wife Katherine died a few weeks later.

The survivors gave thanks for their deliverance, but could hardly be high-spirited. The death toll had been catastrophic.

Among the winter dead – [L] marks a member of the Leyden community:

Mary Norris Allerton (after giving birth to a stillborn child) [L]
Elizabeth Barker
Richard Britteridge [L]
Robert Carter
James Chilton
Susanna Chilton
Richard Clarke [L]
John Craxton (the father) [L]
Sarah Eaton [L]

Moses Fletcher [L]
Anne Fuller [L]
Edward Fuller [L]
John Goodman [L]
William Holbeck [L]
John Hooke [L]
Oceanus Hopkins (the child born at sea)
John Langemore
Edward Margerson [L]
Christopher Martin
Marie Martin
Digerie Priest [L]
Solomon Prower
Thomas Rogers [L]
Rose Standish [L]
Elias Story [L]
Edward Thomson [L]
William White [L]
Thomas Williams [L]

Only four families had escaped the disaster: one of them was that of Stephen and Elizabeth Hopkins, who were not Separatists. In all, just fifty-four of the colonists had survived: thirty Pilgrims and twenty-four Strangers. Twenty-one of these were under the age of 16 – children, really, even in an age when the young were set to work much earlier than we would consider appropriate.

And soon *Mayflower* would be departing, leaving these thirty-three adults and twenty-one children to survive as best they could.

Chapter Eight

Envoi

Mayflower set off on the return journey to England on 5 April 1621, four months after she first made landfall in the New World, under the command of Captain Jones.

Not a single one of the settlers opted to give up and go home. A sceptic might say that this was because they simply could not endure another crossing of the kind that had almost killed them. It would be closer to the truth to say that by now they had fully recovered the faith that God was smiling on their venture, and that better would come, soon.

That faith had been sorely tried and one unhappy consequence of their travails was that the settlers could not expect to make more than a pittance from the fruit of their labours. The returning *Mayflower* carried next to no cargo, because the colony had been too busy merely surviving to produce a surplus. And she was grossly under-manned, since about half the crew had died during the winter's illnesses.

1621: Farming and Thanksgiving.

The colonists elected William Bradford to take over from Carver, even though Bradford was fairly young (31) and almost entirely untried. Moreover, he was one of those who was still seriously ill – so ill that a deputy was appointed to help him cope with the task. No matter: the important thing was he was a direct link with the Pilgrims' idealistic origins back in Scrooby. Bradford would guide the colony well through its earliest years.

It was a hard-working and eventful spring and summer, but at least there was now plenty of fresh and wholesome food – cod and bass fished in abundance from the sea, deer from the woods and, as autumn drew on, duck and turkey. The seeds the Pilgrims had brought from England had not done well, but the maize they had grown under Squanto's direction was plentiful. There was even wine to drink once more, made from the wild grapes they gathered. There were more expeditions, more encounters with Native Americans – including a skirmish in which, it was falsely reported, Squanto had been captured and killed – and some successful trading, which supplied the colonists with a good store of beaver pelts that they sent back to England in 1622 in part-payment for their ever-growing debts to the Merchant Adventurers who were funding the Pilgrims' venture.

Almost everyone knows what happened next. Edward Winslow told the tale, in a book called *Mourt's Relation*, published in 1622:

Our harvest being gotten in, our governor
[Bradford] sent four men on fowling, that
we might after a special manner rejoice
together after we had gathered the fruits
of our labour. They four in one day killed
as much fowl as, with a little help beside,
served the company almost a week. At
which time, amongst other recreations, we
exercised our arms, many of the Indians
coming amongst us, and among the rest
their greatest king Massasoit, with some
ninety men, whom for three days we
entertained and feasted, and they went out
and killed five deer, which we brought
to the plantation and bestowed upon our
governor, and upon the captain [Standish]
and others....

On the 10 November, more colonists arrived – 35 of them,
in a small boat named *Fortune*. Initial joy at the sight of
the newcomers, about a dozen of whom were friends from
Leyden, gave way to disappointment and anger when they
realised that Weston, who had funded this new trip, had
not sent them any fresh provisions or tools along with the
new settlers. With all these new mouths to feed, and the
post-Thanksgiving stores not as abundant as they should
have been, the colony once again faced a hungry winter.
And the following year, there would be a catastrophic turn
in their relationship with some of the Native American
nations.

But those are other stories. The main thing was that they
had survived, and were in the New World to stay. What

happened to the leading players in the years to come?

Captain Jones and Mayflower

Captain Jones returned to his wife and children at their home in Rotherhithe, and spent the remaining months of his life there. He was buried in the local churchyard on 2 March 1622. It is often said that the cause of his early death (he was 52) was a combination of the winter illness of 1621and the sheer strain of bringing *Mayflower* through dangerous seas. It left him a broken man.

The craft herself did not long survive the Captain's death. By 1624 she was a rotting hulk, moored at Rotherhithe near Jones's house. Some local mariners bought what was left of *Mayflower* and chopped her up for timber. She was valued at £128, 8 s 4d: one hundred and twenty-eight pounds, four shillings and fourpence. There are legends that some of her beams were used in the building of churches in Southern England, and there may be truth in them,

John Robinson

The man who had first dreamed of the Pilgrims' journey and inspired them to build a new world died just a few years later, in 1625. Though he remained in the old world, his contribution to the venture and to the way of life they developed in Plymouth was incalculably large.

A plaque set up in Leyden in 1928 by admirers of *Mayflower*'s passengers reads:

In Memory Of

JOHN ROBINSON

Pastor of the English Church in Leyden
1609-1625

His Broadly Tolerant Mind
Guided and Developed the Religious Life of

THE PILGRIMS OF MAYFLOWER

His Broadly Tolerant Mind: Robinson's flock were not bigots.

William Brewster

Brewster died on 18 April 1643. He was seventy-seven – almost a patriarchal age in that century. He had suffered only a single day of illness in his busy life; he gave inspiring and instructive sermons twice every Sunday until his very last weeks; and he had laboured hard in the fields until he grew too weak. Bradford wrote an affectionate farewell to Brewster in his history, noting Brewster's cheerfulness as well as his seriousness, his modesty, his lack of malice and, perhaps above all, his compassion.

Edward Winslow

On 12 May 1621, Winslow married the widow Susana White, who had lost her husband William; it was the first marriage celebrated in the colony, and it was a civil marriage, because the Separatists could find no satisfactory warrant in Scripture for a religious ceremony. He became one of the most influential leaders in Plymouth, and served three terms as governor, but he was not to die in America.

In 1646, Winslow returned to England to aid Oliver Cromwell and the English Revolution. Three years later, when Charles I was executed, he considered returning to Plymouth, but was persuaded that his first duty was to the Commonwealth, and he stayed. In 1655 he took part in British naval action against Spain, in the Caribbean. The British won, but Winslow caught yellow fever and died, not far from the coast of Jamaica, on 7 May.

Miles Standish

Officially, Standish continued to be the colony's military commander until his death on 3 October 1656, little more than a year after Winslow's death at sea. In reality, he spent the last few years of his life rather more peaceably, working his own land. Standish was a colourful figure who prompted argument, both in his lifetime and ever since. On the one hand he was unquestionably brave, loyal to his fellows and a good military strategist. On the other he was reckless, favoured a ethically dubious policy of pre-emptive attacks, and could be shockingly brutal, to a degree that angered the Native Americans and gave pause to other Pilgrims.

His fame today owes much to the fanciful account of his romantic life written by the poet Longfellow in 1858: *The Courtship of Miles Standish*. Longfellow's book is probably the single most influential contribution to popular mythology about Pilgrim life – above all, in mixing up the Pilgrims and the Puritans as if they were one and the same people.

William Bradford

Bradford died on 9 May 1657. He was 68, and had spent the better part of the last 36 years as governor. (His periods in office were: 1621-32; 1635; 1637; 1639-43; and 1645 until his death). He governed so long not because he had a lust for power, but because his fellows believed he was the right man for the job, and because he repeatedly showed that they had chosen their leader wisely. The odd and untried boy from Nottinghamshire had matured, through adversity, into a natural leader.

From the point of view of posterity, Bradford's accomplishment in steering his people is rivalled by the importance of his major work of history. Though it is often misleadingly referred to as a journal, *Of Plymouth Plantation* was written in retrospect. He began it in 1630, put the task aside for a few years, and then resumed it between 1646 and 1650. He never completed the book, which ends with an account of the major events of 1646.

The manuscript of Bradford's history was lost some time around 1680, and was presumably taken as loot by an unusually literate English soldier, since it turned up again on the other side of the Atlantic, when it was discovered in the library of Lambeth Palace in London.

Bradford was never much given to exultation, so it is worth noting that the one time he was moved to rejoicing was when he heard news of the English Civil War, and the triumph of Cromwell's forces:

> Rejoice, yea and again rejoice, and say
> Hallelujah, salvation, and glory, and
> honour, and power to the Lord our God,
> for true and righteous are his judgements.
> Hallelujah!

Bradford wrote much more about theology than about politics, as we understand the term, but this shout of triumph shows that he thought that the Pilgrim mission in America and the coming of a Revolution in England were two parts of one great historical movement. God, evidently, was well pleased with both methods of freeing the English of their monarchs.

Chapter Nine

Hindsight

A great deal has been written about the Pilgrims as the founders of a country that, a century and a half later, would become the United States in America. Some of this colossal output is fanciful, but there are certain irreducible truths that will stand up to the most searching scrutiny. One of them is that the survival of Plymouth was a vast encouragement to other English dissenters who were considering emigration, and that New England became the favoured destination for those non-conforming Protestants who preferred fleeing from Kings to cutting off royal heads.

Writing at a time (1957) when the "English-Speaking Peoples" were again largely confident that God – or at any rate Right – was on their side, Winston Churchill took a visionary long view of the years that followed the landing of *Mayflower:*

> In these first decades of the great
> emigration, over eighty thousand
> English speaking people crossed the
> Atlantic. Never since the days of the
> Germanic invasions of Britain had
> such a national movement been seen.
> Saxon and Viking had colonised Britain.
> Now, one thousand years later, their
> descendants were taking possession
> of America.

All of which had been, Churchill thought, a magnificent achievement. Few historians would write in such a confident and sweeping manner today, and not only because we look with far more distress on what the English settlers in the New World eventually did to its original inhabitants. Yet even with this sense of gross injustice in mind, it is hard not to admire the Plymouth Pilgrims, not only for their courage and resourcefulness but for other virtues, too.

Quite apart from their accomplishment in simply staying alive, the Pilgrims found a way to accommodate the Strangers' potentially disruptive and dissenting attitudes in a community that was not merely obedient to its own laws but civil and mannerly; *e pluribus unum*. Again, though they were plainly not democrats in the modern sense, their meetings set democratic precedents that would be remembered in later years.

Where most other colonial ventures from Spain and England had been glorified looting parties, ruthless armed grabs for territory and gold, the Pilgrims' major worldly ambition was to cultivate the earth and to trade with their neighbours on terms of peace and amity. Unlike the Bay

Puritans who followed them, they did not allow their firm views on religion to harden into persecutory fanaticism. And they enjoyed their cakes and ale.

How did the *Mayflower* voyage shape these intrepid men and women? Profoundly, though in ways that are not always easy to specify. Long before setting out, they had thought of themselves as a special type of people, set apart from the common run of mankind and sworn enemies of Satan who ruled most of the world. Their God had tested them sorely, but they had passed the test, and though there were more trials to come, they were now all the more certain that He smiled on their purposes. Page after page of Bradford's history affirms the workings of Divine Providence.

Hardship and disaster can turn people into feral animals, out only for their own survival, or they can bring out better instincts. The Pilgrims went down the latter path, to such an extent that they even won the grudging respect of *Mayflower*'s coarsest crew members. At their moments of greatest peril, the Pilgrims showed a compassion so intense and so self-sacrificing as to inspire admiration more than four centuries later.

In these respects, they were heroes.

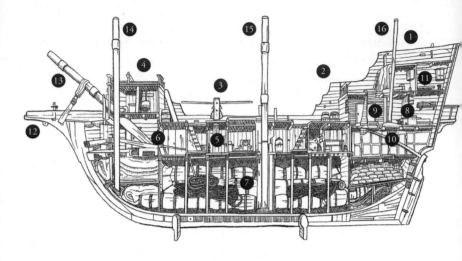

There are no surviving plans for the Mayflower, and the diagrams shown here have been deduced from the likely layout of the ship based upon similar Elizabethan vessels of the day. This cutaway view shows where the passengers, crew and supplies would have been packed into the Mayflower for the 1620 crossing.

1. Poop deck
2. Half deck
3. Upper deck
4. Forecastle
5. Main deck where most of the pilgrims were housed
6. Crew's quarters
7. Large hold
8. Special cabins

9. Helmsman with whipstaff controlling the tiller
10. Tiller room
11. Captain's cabin
12. Beak
13. Bowsprit
14. Foremast
15. Mainmast
16. Mizzen mast

Ship cross section courtesy of © Jack Merton and Illuminate Rotherhithe www.illuminaterotherhithe.co.uk
Plans to the right courtesy of Best Ship Models www.bestshipmodels.com

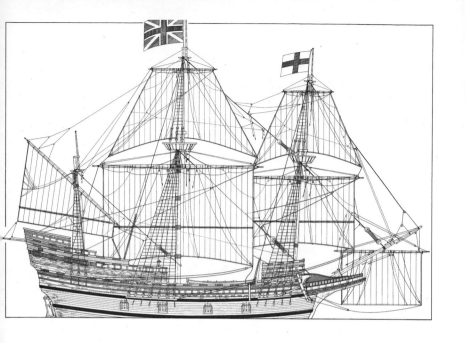

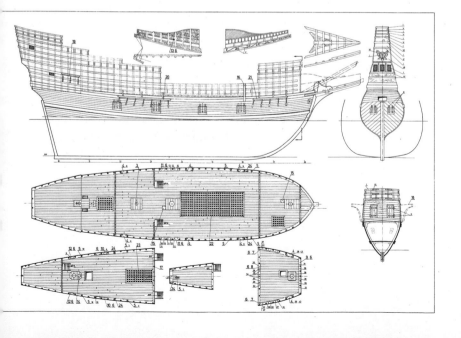

The Queen's Pirate:
Sir Francis Drake & the Golden Hind

The Queen's Pirate: Sir Francis Drake & the Golden Hind
tells the extraordinary story of Drake's early years and his
journey around the world on his famous ship, the Golden
Hind. For more than four centuries, Drake has been world-
famous for his feats as a master mariner – the captain who
"singed the King of Spain's beard" with his daredevil attack
on the fleet at Cadiz, and who led the British Navy to
victory against the Spanish Armada in 1588. But Drake's
exploits in his earlier years, though less well known, are
even more remarkable. Born into a poor, obscure family,
he worked his way rapidly up in the maritime world to his
first captaincy. Before long, he was the most successful of
all English pirates, admired by his countrymen, hated and
feared by the Spanish. Queen Elizabeth saw the potential in
this rough-mannered but enterprising young man, and gave
him her blessing for the first British venture into the Pacific
Ocean. This success of this voyage, which lasted for three
years, exceeded their wildest hopes. Not only did Drake
come home with a vast treasure of captured gold, silver and
jewels; he became the first man ever to circumnavigate the
globe in a single mission, and bring most of his crew home
alive and well.

THE Queen's Pirate

SEVEN SHIPS · MARITIME HISTORY

SIR FRANCIS DRAKE &
THE GOLDEN HIND

KEVIN JACKSON

Chapter One

A Tree in Darien

It was the mid-morning of 11 February 1573, the sun intensely bright and the day already growing uncomfortably warm and muggy. The English sea-captain and pirate Mr Francis Drake – he would not be *Sir* Francis until 1580 – was making his way westwards on foot through the pine forests of Panama, with plunder in mind. His plan was to make a surprise attack on one of more of the Spanish mule trains that were carrying immense amounts of gold and silver from mines in Peru, so that it could be put on board treasure ships and sent back to Spain, which was now the most powerful country in the Western world.

With him was a small company from his ship's crew. At the age of 33, Drake was a good two decades older than most of his shipmates – 18 very young men and boys, most of them from his own county of Devon, in the southwest of England. They were, in effect, a band of guerrillas, passing stealthily through enemy territory, since Spanish forces had almost complete possession of this country.

The English force was attended by a band of friendly, reliable native guides, all ferociously hostile to the Spanish colonists in Panama and, thus, delighted to join Drake's expeditionary team. They were known as "Cimaroons". It had been six exhausting days since the team had set out from their ship's mooring on the Atlantic coastline, and the march had mostly been uphill, first through wet, steamy jungle, now through trees.

Spanish warships patrolled the Atlantic seaboard, behind them, and there was a large Spanish garrison ahead of them, in Panama City. They had to move stealthily, sending a couple of Cimaroons ahead to scout. If they encountered anyone, the scouts would run back and the expedition would vanish into the depths of the forest before anyone could spot them and raise the alarm. The English boys carried nothing but their arms, since the Cimaroons had generously insisted on carrying all the other kit and provisions. The lads were under strict orders not to kill women, children, or unarmed men, and also to enforce this rule on their guides, who would willingly have massacred Spaniards of any age or sex.

The march had fallen into a daily routine. It was much too hot to move in the middle hours of the day, so they walked in the early mornings and late evenings, making camp at night when it was refreshingly cool. Drake had used their midnight rests as a chance to teach the Cimaroons the Lord's Prayer in English, but without much success.

As they pushed upwards through the pines, the chief of their Cimaroon escort, a man they knew by the name the Spanish had given him, "Pedro", suddenly called a halt, and pointed forward. Drake peered through the dense covering trees, and could just make out that a short walk ahead of them was a slightly higher peak, marking the watershed of the Cordilleras. This was the landmark he had hoped to find.

Encouraged by this discovery, the company pushed on with renewed vigour, and soon had climbed the peak. Here, Pedro took Drake by the hand, and led him to a tall tree. Drake noticed that steps had been cut into its body, and that high up among the branches was a look-out platform, large enough for about a dozen men to stand on. Pedro climbed the steps, and Drake followed. He looked around.

Behind him to the East, he could see the Atlantic Ocean. To the West…well, he knew at once that it was the "Southern Ocean" or the "Secret Ocean", that much-discussed but largely unknown mass of water that Magellan had called "the Pacific". No Englishman had ever enjoyed this simultaneous vista of both oceans; nor had many Europeans. Among that select number, sixty years earlier, was Vasco Nunez de Balboa, the Spanish commander at Darien, who had climbed the very same tree in 1513. Centuries later, the English Romantic poet John Keats evoked that vision in one of his most famous sonnets, "On First Looking Into Chapman's Homer" – though Keats made a famous blunder, wrongly identifying the bold explorer not as Balboa but as Cortez:

Then felt I like some watcher of the skies
When a new planet sweeps into his ken;
Or like stout Cortez when with eagle eyes
He stared at the Pacific – and all his men
Looked at each other with a wild surmise
– Silent, upon a peak in Darien.

The records tell us that Balboa, a good Catholic and patriotic Spaniard, had at once prayed to God and the Blessed Virgin Mary to "give him good success to subdue these lands to the glory of His name and the increase of the true religion." Accompanied by his men, he marched down to the waterfront, waded up to his waist into the sea, raised his sword and his shield and asked for the company to bear witness that he had taken possession of the ocean – "and all that appertains to it" – for the King of Castile and Leon.

Balboa's water-grab for Spain had remained unchallenged by any other nation, and Spanish rule of the Pacific was all but absolute. But Drake had other ideas. This sea, he fervently believed, ought to be the property of his country and his Queen, Elizabeth I. Like Balboa before him, Drake fell to his knees, thanked Almighty God for this miraculous vision, and prayed to Him to make it possible to sail across these new waters some day soon as captain of an English ship.

Then he summoned up the other English men and boys so that they could share this wonderful view, and he told them about his prayers for a great adventure into the Pacific. One of the company, John Oxenham, vowed that "unless our Captain did beat him from his company, he would follow him by God's grace."

From that point on, Drake was a man in the grip of an obsession. He vowed that one day he would sail into the Pacific, and wrest it from the hands of Spain.

Chapter Two

Enter the Dragon

The Spanish, who started to pay attention to the danger posed by this upstart English pirate some time in the early 1570s, knew him by several names: *Diaz*; *Draq*; *El Draque*. But in the long run he was most commonly known as *El Draco*: The Dragon. By the time Sir Francis Drake played his triumphant part in the defeat on the Spanish Armada in 1588 – one of the truly decisive significant sea battles in British history – they identified their deadly enemy as the Devil himself. Only diabolic agency, they believed, could account for his triumphs.

Born into obscure and humble circumstances, he had become the most famous man in the Western world. Drake's life ranks with that of Napoleon as one of the dozen or so most astonishing rags-to-riches stories of the last thousand years. And though he reached his prime in age of great English explorers and warriors – Sir Walter Raleigh, Sir Martin Frobisher, Sir Philip Sidney – Drake was the brightest star in that Elizabethan firmament.

Nobody else came close.

His countrymen adored him, not simply because he captured or sank so many enemy ships, nor because he brought home vast quantities of gold and silver, but for the sheer dash and audacity with which he carried out his raids. They saw in him their own image -- or an image of what they might be, at their best. His enemies came to dread him. Spanish sailors were terrified whenever they heard that Drake was sailing against them; while Spanish mothers at home would frighten their children into obedience by telling them that the English Devil would come and eat them.

The myth of Drake, already potent in his own lifetime, grew and grew from the early seventeenth century onwards, when propagandists for the rise of British sea power set him up as the chief exemplar of daring, enterprise, patriotism, Protestantism and military genius. The process began in his lifetime, and gathered momentum in 1628, with the publication of *The World Encompassed by Sir Francis Drake* – a narrative of the circumnavigation compiled from notes made by Francis Fletcher, who was chaplain on the expedition. It urged young Englishman to give up their foppish and effete ways, and to model themselves on their nation's hero.

Not until the time of Nelson, more than two centuries later, was there a sailor to rival him in his country's admiration. Many of the things that were said of him were in large part fanciful, such as the charming but almost certainly false yarn that he carried on nonchalantly playing a game of bowls when he first had word of the Armada sailing up the English Channel. It hardly matters: the story struck a deep chord in the English imagination. One of the country's deepest legends is that Arthur and his Knights are sleeping in a cave somewhere, ready to wake up and do battle when Britain is in peril; a national myth of the Victorian era reassured his countrymen that Drake's drum will pound out a loud warning when the enemy is approaching.

The patriotic myth of Drake reached its peak in the nineteenth century, when Britain possessed the global empire that Queen Elizabeth's magician, Dr John Dee, had both predicted and planned. But the legend survived, in milder forms, well into the twentieth and twenty-first centuries. Until recently, one of the standard British coins carried an image of the *Golden Hind*, the small ship in which Drake circumnavigated the world from 1577-1580.

Not until the last few decades, when indignation at all forms of colonialism has grown fierce and widespread, did anyone suggest that his violent aggressions were anything other than bold and thrilling adventures. Today's students of history are more likely to see him as a gangster and a thug: highly successful at his own types of crime, no more.

And yet no amount of historical revisionism can make him seem insignificant. By any reckoning, Drake was a remarkable man, and an exceptionally brave one; possibly the greatest navigator of his age; a military strategist of impulsive, untutored genius; and a visionary, venturesome soul. This was the age when England, which had declined from its former power just a couple of centuries earlier into a somewhat poor and minor kingdom off the coast of continental Europe. In the Western, the big powers were France, Portugal and, above all, Spain. Under Elizabeth, the English began to dream again of wealth and power. Drake was the man who might make those dreams come true.

Darwin's Odyssey:
The Voyage of the Beagle

The young Charles Darwin was like a young Indiana Jones. For five years in his mid-twenties, he sailed on the Beagle around the world, exploring jungles, climbing mountains, trekking across deserts. With every new landfall, he had new adventures: he rode through bandit country, was thrown into jail by revolutionaries, took part in an armed raid with marines, survived two earthquakes, hunted and fished. He suffered the terrible cold and rain of Tierra del Fuego, the merciless heat of the Australian outback and the inner pangs of heartbreak. He also made the discoveries that finally led him to formulate his theory of Natural Selection as the driving force of evolution. The five-year voyage of the Beagle was the basis for all Darwin's later work; but it also turned him from a friendly idler into the greatest scientist of his century.

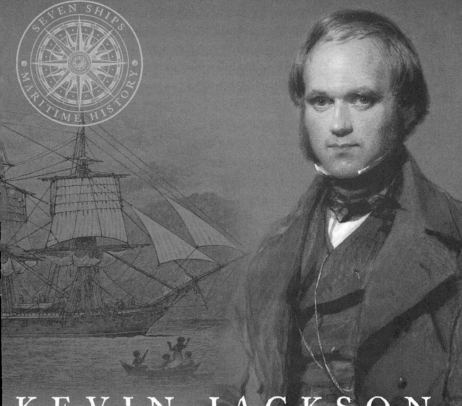

Darwin's
Odyssey

THE VOYAGE OF THE BEAGLE

SEVEN SHIPS
MARITIME HISTORY

KEVIN JACKSON

Prologue: The Calm after the Storms

C harles Darwin had endured thirty years of constant hard and often agonisingly dull work. He had been dogged by chronic illness – blinding headaches, agonising stomach cramps, eczema, palpitations, giddiness, and a daily, sometimes hourly, compulsion to vomit. Sometimes these pains were exacerbated by bouts of severe depression that rendered him all but incapable of movement or speech. Melancholy was something that ran in his family, but Charles suffered it more than most of the Darwins, not least in the unbearable months after his most beloved daughter, Annie, died at the age of ten. In middle life he had grown ever more timid, and at times somewhat reclusive. Almost morbidly afraid of offending anyone, and aware that when his alarming theories about the mutability of species were made public many people would be outraged, he had delayed making his conclusions know for twenty years. Another reason for his delay was caution and self-doubt: he wanted to be entirely certain that each of the points he wished to make could be supported by a body of evidence so massive as to be overwhelming. This process had included eight full years engrossed in a minute study of thousands and thousands of barnacles. A distant branch of our family tree.

Gradually, though, at around the start of the 1870s and until his final days, Charles's mood began to lighten. Other, more pugnacious men like his close friend Thomas Huxley had fought the good fight on his behalf. A large part of the civilized world now knew his name, and though angry voices were still raised against him, he was a hero to the thoughtful classes of every nation. Evolution, once an insult to humanity, was now not merely tolerated but enthusiastically embraced by some of the most powerful men and women in the world. Honors poured in from Europe and America, and he was elected to more than sixty learned societies. He was prosperous, powerful, and quietly proud of his accomplishments.

Moreover, as Charles's anxieties decreased, his health improved – strong evidence that the symptoms which had made his life a purgatory for three decades must have been nervous rather than organic in origin. He had always doted on his wife Emma and his children, when breaks from his almost unrelenting labors gave him time for domestic affection. Now he could enjoy their company more frequently and with less divided attention. In later years, they would recall his sweet, gentle nature with fondness. The shy, self-tormenting invalid had become a Victorian patriarch and benevolent squire. And he had changed mankind's view of the world more profoundly than any scientist since Copernicus. More profoundly, perhaps, than any scientist before or since – because the battles for and against his dangerous discovery involved hot emotion as well as cool intellect.

None of this would have happened had he turned down an offer that came to him when he was a hearty, healthy, apparently lazy young man of twenty-two summers.

Chapter 1

Charles the Idler

D r Robert Darwin was angry with his youngest son, Charles. It was the summer of 1831, and the youngest of the Darwin boys looked as if her was wasting his life. "You care for nothing but shooting, dogs and rat-catching, and you will be a disgrace to yourself and all your family", the Doctor shouted at Charles. Many years later, looking back on this outburst, Charles had to agree that his father had not been exaggerating: "He was very properly vehement against my turning [into] an idle sporting man, which then seemed my probable destination ..."

As far as Dr Darwin could see, his son was a three-time failure, who had daydreamed his way through school, dropped out of a medical course in Edinburgh and then spent most of his time at Cambridge riding and hunting by day and drinking and gambling at night. He was not, perhaps, downright stupid, but neither was he all that clever. Charles recalled years later in his *Autobiography*: "I believe I was considered by all my masters and by my

Father as a very ordinary boy, rather below the common standard in intellect."

More dismaying than his sub-average mental ability was Charles's refusal to settle down to pursue a gentlemanly profession. Guessing that neither the Army nor the Law would suit Charles, Dr Darwin lit on the final alternative for the sons of the prosperous: he wanted him to become a clergyman. Charles made only mild objections to this plan, but he was making no effort to study the works of theology that he would need to master. In the summer months following his graduation from Cambridge in 1831 he had done little else but loll around the family house or venture out to destroy large quantities of rural wildlife with his gun.

In many respects, Dr Darwin was quite right. Charles had indeed idled at his formal studies, he had not shown many signs of mental acuity, and he was not burning with ambition to become a parson. But what his father had not noticed was how passionately Charles had been pursuing his "hobbies" – entomology, botany, geology and other aspects of natural history. At most, Dr Darwin thought that the undemanding life of a parson would give his son plenty of leisure time to enjoy such pursuits; indeed, some of England's leading naturalists were clergymen. Many of the country's scientists were still, as they had been for generations, gentleman (and occasionally lady) amateurs – wealthy in their own right, or blessed with virtual sine-cures. It would have astonished him to learn that his son would become respected around the world as the greatest naturalist of his century, or of all time. Fortunately, he lived long enough to take pride in some of his son's astounding accomplishments.

By a quirk of history, Charles Darwin was born on the same day as another giant figure of the nineteenth century, Abraham Lincoln: 12 February 1809. Charles's grandfather, Erasmus Darwin (1731–1802), had been a famous man of his day, not only as a highly successful medical doctor but also as a "natural philosopher" – the word "scientist" had not yet been coined – and a poet, who used verse as the medium for advancing his various theories. Erasmus, a humane and agreeable man, had propounded a theory of evolution – in fact, one of the most famous of the theories of evolution that had been in the air during the late eighteenth century.

Erasmus Darwin's third son, Robert Waring Darwin (1766–1848), dutifully followed the course set out for him by his father and, after medical studies in Edinburgh and Leyden, settled in the provincial town of Shrewsbury, about 160 miles from London, soon established himself as a prosperous physician and shrewd businessman, and went on to become one of the wealthiest men in the county. Some of his success was due to his unusually sensitive bedside manner. He discovered that quite a few of his patients would get better if he simply sat quietly and listened to them – an antecedent of later types of "talking cure".

Robert Darwin built The Mount, a large house near the river, and in 1796 married Susannah Wedgwood, the oldest daughter of Josiah Wedgwood. The Wedgwood family had grown rich and world famous from their pottery manufacturing business, and there had long been social close ties between the two families, who were also related. They shared Whig politics, supported reforming causes and were ardent voices in the battle against the slave trade. Charles maintained these political allegiances throughout his life.

As a young boy, Charles was doted on by his two older sisters, who grew ever more protective and possessive of him after his mother died in June 1817, when he was eight years old. Some biographers have speculated that this early experience of loss was at the root of the many illnesses that afflicted him from his thirties onwards; but others have argued that he was given more than enough affection to see him through his bereavement, and that while it is probable that his torments were psychosomatic, their cause needs to be sought elsewhere – perhaps in his early guilt at disappointing a father who had made high demands of him.

In the year his mother died, Charles began to attend a day school nearby, and in 1818 went on to Dr Butler's School in Shrewsbury, where he remained until he was sixteen. The curriculum at Dr Butler's establishment, like that of most British schools of the day, was almost exclusively classical: hours and hours of Latin and Greek, leavened only slightly by ancient Geography and History. Charles, already a keen amateur naturalist, was bored to distraction and, as noted, did not shine in the class-room. Outside the school walls he was a different boy: he would fish, collect shells and other specimens, and go on long solitary walks, fantasizing about the exotic islands and forests he had read about in children's books such as *Wonders of the World*. He and his older brother Erasmus, usually called "Eras", also set up their own laboratory in the garden shed. When Charles's schoolmates heard about the noxious fumes that the brothers were creating, they gave him the nickname "Gas". When he was fifteen Charles was given his first gun, and he discovered that he loved shooting at birds so much that he would actually tremble with excitement. Within a year or so, his love began to border on the obsessive: "How I did enjoy shooting ... If there is bliss on earth, that is it ... My zeal was so great that I used to place my shooting-boots open by my bed-side when I went to bed, so as not to lose half-a-minute in putting them on in the morning."

Dr Darwin had resolved that his two sons should continue the family tradition and become medical practitioners, so when Charles was sixteen he was sent to Edinburgh to join his brother at the University. Erasmus eventually qualified as a doctor, but never practiced, instead living comfortably on an allowance from their father and cutting an elegant figure as a bachelor in the more fashionable districts of London. Charles never completed his studies, partly because he found many of the lectures tedious, but also because he found the dissection of corpses distressing, and the sight of operations – carried out without the blessing of anesthetics, with the screams of patients rending the air – simply terrifying. When he saw a child being operated on in this brutal, bloody fashion, he ran out of the operating theatre and vowed never to return.

Getting wind of this slackening of attention, Dr Darwin suspected that Charles was losing his way again, and was furious: "If you continue your present indulgent way, your course of study will be utterly useless." Again, it was fair comment, at least as far as medical training was concerned. In reality, though, the teenage Darwin was educating himself very well in other areas. He spent hours wandering along the nearby coast with his brother, collecting marine specimens. He and Eras both read deeply and widely in many subjects, above all in Natural History. He also acquitted himself of an invaluable practical skill: "I am going to learn to stuff birds, from a blackamoor."

Today we find this epithet offensive, but, far from being disdainful of his new teacher, a former slave by the name of John Edmonstone, Charles reported that he found the older man charming company and highly intelligent. It confirmed the slogan that appeared on a famous image used by the abolitionist movement that he had known from his earliest days: it showed a slave kneeling in chains, and asking "Am I not a man and a brother?" When later in life he met people of other races during his trip around the globe, Darwin took it for granted that they were likely to be as intelligent as any English person, and was happy to concede that some other peoples, such as the Tahitians, were healthier, happier and more beautiful than most white people. Charles also loved hearing about Edmonstone's experiences of tropical countries, which revived his boyhood dreams of travel to hot lands.

Charles passed his second and what was to be his final year in Edinburgh alone, since Eras was pursuing further studies in London. He found the place lonely without his brother, so threw himself into an assortment of extra-curricular activities: he joined various societies, notably the Plinian which hosted talks about science, radical politics and religion. He also found the first important mentor of his life in Dr Robert Grant, a former medical practitioner who had turned his powerful intellect to marine biology, and was a loud and brilliant proponent of evolutionary theory. Darwin had already learned about evolution from his grandfather's writings, but Grant introduced him to the full blast of the revolutionary theories coming out of France, particularly those of Lamarck and St Hilaire. Charles went on long walks with Grant, came to know him well, and caught his intellectual fervor for sea-slugs and sponges.

Grant was pursing an intensive study of marine invertebrates which would very soon establish him as one of the leading scientists in the field. Darwin followed in his footsteps, literally as well as figuratively, and with Grant to guide him began his own marine researches. By the early months of 1827, he was beginning to make small but not insignificant discoveries of his own. Darwin also began to take an interest in geology, and sat in on lectures given by the famous geologist Robert Jameson, which he found fascinating despite the dreariness of their delivery. By the end of his time in Edinburgh, he had learned how to dissect animals, stuff and mount them, and use a microscope. He was entranced by the sights it revealed.

But he had not learned much medicine. In the early summer of 1827 he set off on travels around the country and made his first and last visit to Europe – a short trip to Paris, reluctantly funded by his father. Upon returning to The Mount, Charles threw himself into hunting and socializing. He particularly enjoyed visiting Woodhouse, the country estate of Mr William Mostyn Owen, which was just a short ride away from Shrewsbury. Mr Owen liked Charles, and took the young man with him on long country rambles during which they would shoot hares and birds, talk liberal politics and gossip about family and friends. Compared to the quiet gloom of The Mount, Woodhouse was a place of delicious chaos, large and noisy dinners and hearty drinking. It also offered an additional attraction: Owen's pretty young daughters. Charles's eye was particularly caught by Fanny Owen, a year his senior. Mr Owen was pleased by Charles's obvious interest in Fanny: he had four daughters to marry off soon, and Charles was a fine fellow – excellent son-in-law material.

Fanny was a charming girl, and certainly not a shy one. She flirted, loved attending dances and was almost exhaustingly cheerful. Soon, Charles was entirely smitten; it is hard to tell how she felt about him. They began a correspondence in which her imaginative flights, word-play and teasing seem to teeter on the edge of *double entendre*, but they may have been entirely innocent of serious flirtation. Many years later, one of Charles's sons saw the blissful expression on his father's face as he reminisced about seeing Fanny handle a gun like a true sportsman, and concluded that this must have been the exact moment when Darwin realized he was in love. Love meant marriage, though; and to be married, a young man really ought to have a profession.

Since Robert Darwin had abandoned his well-inten-tioned efforts to coax his son back into medicine, he urged Charles to consider entering the Church or risk finding himself cut off from all financial support. This choice of career may seem almost insane in the light of the damage Darwin's mature work was to inflict on the faithful of many creeds, but Darwin was at this time a believing – if not particularly pious –Anglican and would remain so for years to come. (He was mildly shocked when he first met a man who did not believe in the literal truth of the story of the Flood in Genesis.) Charles hesitated a while, flipped through a few recent books on the Christian faith that quieted the few minor qualms he had about the orthodoxy of his views, and agreed to do what his father said.

At this time, the road to Holy Orders included a degree, so Charles was dispatched to Cambridge, where he matriculated in January 1828 following an intensive period of cramming Greek with a private tutor – for he discovered that he had forgotten absolutely all the Greek he had learned at Butler's School. There was not a free room for him in his college, Christ's, so he lodged for his first terms in a small apartment above a nearby tobacconist's shop. His Cambridge studies would not tax him unduly; he read just enough to scrape by, and otherwise did as he pleased – making new friends, learning to drink (this was the only period of his life when he was in the habit of hearty drinking) and indulging in long reveries about Fanny.

He also discovered a new and to him wholly absorbing pastime: beetles. Throughout his undergraduate days, Darwin's chief pleasure was to head off into the nearby countryside and hunt for specimens, which he also learned to mount. Within two years, he was skilled and learned enough to be able to hold his own in the company of Britain's most eminent entomologists, and he was named in a scholarly journal as the finder of an unknown species. This gave him, he said, the same kind of thrill a poet feels when he sees his first verses in print.

Britain was in a state of intense political turmoil during Darwin's Cambridge years, and his university town was not immune. Angered by what they viewed as the tyranny of University discipline, students rioted, much as the students of the 1960s would do in the following century. Though Charles was seldom directly involved, his sympathy lay with the rebels. And if he was not an open rebel, he was something of a truant, often breaking the nightly curfew; a misdemeanor that put him in some risk of "rustication": being expelled either for a term or for good. He was growing increasingly despondent about his romance with Fanny, who now seldom replied to his letters, and for long periods fell into a state of gloom; nothing like as bad as the depressions that tortured him in later life, but enough to make him discontented.

Science rescued him. He became deeply interested in the lectures on Botany given by Professor John Stevens Henslow (1796–1861), and before long he was eagerly joining Henslow on field trips – on foot, by coach, or on barges drifting down the rivers Granta and Cam, to examine plants and animals and to enjoy Henslow's discourses. The two men became close friends, and Charles often joined Henslow and his family for dinners. Henslow encouraged Charles to revive his former interest in geology by attending a series of lectures given by Professor Sedgwick. He did so, and was almost instantly converted. It delighted him to see how superbly Sedgwick could teach the subject to beginners. He would take parties out on long rides through the countryside, point out details and fire their imaginations rather than cramming them with facts. Geology, botany and entomology were now the intellectual loves of Charles's life.

Towards the end of his undergraduate days, Charles discovered a book which excited him more than anything he had ever read: Alexander von Humboldt's *Personal Narrative* of his five-year journey through the forests of Brazil (1799–1804); he found it so enthralling and so finely written that he began to dream of making his own expedition. To be exact, he set about trying to organize a scientific mission in Tenerife, about which von Humboldt had rhapsodized, accompanied by a few student friends ... and financed by indulgent parents. He worked himself up to such a pitch of excitement that he could hardly sit still, and set out doggedly to learn some Spanish. When not studying, he would sit under a palm tree in Cambridge's botanical gardens, daydreaming about the tropics.

On other matters, he had reason enough to be moody and anxious. Mr Owen had broken the news to him that Fanny had become engaged. It was a bad blow, but as long as she remained unmarried he would not abandon hope. In the meantime, there was the small matter of final examinations.

Charles sat his finals in January 1831, after a few weeks of rapid cramming. He came tenth in his class of 178 passes – a most creditable result after three years largely spent chasing beetles. Cambridge's unusual regulations on residence meant that he had to stay on in town until June, indulging in fantasies about adventures in Tenerife. Meanwhile, Henslow had persuaded Professor Sedgwick to take Charles with him on his annual field trip – the next one being to North Wales.

Charles went home for the early summer, and after some difficult talks father and son came to an understanding. Charles agreed that he would return to Cambridge in October 1831 to begin the studies in Divinity that would pave the path towards priesthood; and Robert allowed his son to enjoy the leisurely long vacation without further argument. He also gave him £200 to pay off his Cambridge debts and, implicitly, to help with the finances of the proposed Tenerife expedition.

He spent most of August in Wales with Sedgwick, receiving a crash course in the elements of geological fieldwork by one of the men best qualified to teach the subject. Sedgwick had two principal aims in mind. First he wanted to check on, and where necessary improve, the details of a geological survey that had been made about a decade earlier, and which he suspected had been rendered out of date by the rapid advances that had taken place in the subject during those years. Second – for reasons that were both scientific and religious – he wanted to examine the fossil record of the area, and to disprove, if he could, a recent contention that fossil deposits provided no evidence that life on earth had passed through successive stages from simple to complex forms. Sedgwick, as pious as he was brilliant, believed that the fossil record was God's writing in the rocks. Sedwick taught Charles several key lessons. He showed the young man how to "read" a landscape – to recognise how certain types of vegetation and other features pointed to specific underlying formations. He showed Charles how to make diagrams of rock sections, how to mark up a map with geological detail, how to measure escarpments, and how to gather fossils and grasp their significance. In a broader sense, he showed Charles the rudiments of how to think like a geologist.

For the rest of his life, Charles was deeply grateful to Sedgwick for this invaluable training. He returned home to The Mount on 29 August, his head still fizzing with all the skills and knowledge that had been crammed into him. Immediately ahead of him was the agreeable prospect of two weeks of shooting with his uncle; then in October he would go back to Cambridge, do just enough work for his future career in the Church, and start planning the Tenerife trip in earnest. In the event, none of this would happen.

There was a letter waiting for him.